FREE Test Taking Tips Video/DVD Offer

To better serve you, we created videos covering test taking tips that we want to give you for FREE. **These videos cover world-class tips that will help you succeed on your test.**

We just ask that you send us feedback about this product. Please let us know what you thought about it—whether good, bad, or indifferent.

To get your **FREE videos**, you can use the QR code below or email freevideos@studyguideteam.com with "Free Videos" in the subject line and the following information in the body of the email:

    a. The title of your product

    b. Your product rating on a scale of 1-5, with 5 being the highest

    c. Your feedback about the product

If you have any questions or concerns, please don't hesitate to contact us at info@studyguideteam.com.

Thank you!

GMAT Focus Edition Prep 2024 and 2025
2 Practice Tests and GMAT Study Guide Book [Updated for the New Exam Outline]

Lydia Morrison

Copyright © 2024 by TPB Publishing

All rights reserved. No part of this publication may be reproduced, distributed, or transmitted in any form or by any means, including photocopying, recording, or other electronic or mechanical methods, without the prior written permission of the publisher, except in the case of brief quotations embodied in critical reviews and certain other noncommercial uses permitted by copyright law.

Written and edited by TPB Publishing.

TPB Publishing is not associated with or endorsed by any official testing organization. TPB Publishing is a publisher of unofficial educational products. All test and organization names are trademarks of their respective owners. Content in this book is included for utilitarian purposes only and does not constitute an endorsement by TPB Publishing of any particular point of view.

Interested in buying more than 10 copies of our product? Contact us about bulk discounts:
bulkorders@studyguideteam.com

ISBN 13: 9781637750469

Table of Contents

Welcome --- 1
   FREE Videos/DVD OFFER --- 1
Quick Overview --- 2
Test-Taking Strategies --- 3
Introduction to the GMAT Focus Edition --- 7
Study Prep Plan for the GMAT Focus Edition --- 9
Quantitative Reasoning --- 10
   Arithmetic and Algebra --- 10
   Problem Solving --- 26
Verbal Reasoning --- 27
   Reading Comprehension --- 27
   Critical Reasoning --- 33
Data Insights --- 37
   Data Sufficiency --- 37
   Graphics Interpretation --- 38
   Multi-Source Reasoning --- 44
   Two-Part Analysis --- 48
Practice Test #1 --- 49
   Quantitative Reasoning --- 49
   Verbal Reasoning --- 53
   Data Insights --- 60
Answer Explanations #1 --- 72
   Quantitative Reasoning --- 72

Verbal Reasoning --- 75

Data Insights -- 81

Practice Test #2 -- *86*

Quantitative Reasoning --- 86

Verbal Reasoning --- 90

Data Insights -- 99

Answer Explanations #2 ----------------------------------- *110*

Quantitative Reasoning --- 110

Verbal Reasoning --- 114

Data Insights -- 120

Index --- *125*

Welcome

Dear Reader,

Welcome to your new Test Prep Books study guide! We are pleased that you chose us to help you prepare for your exam. There are many study options to choose from, and we appreciate you choosing us. Studying can be a daunting task, but we have designed a smart, effective study guide to help prepare you for what lies ahead.

Whether you're a parent helping your child learn and grow, a high school student working hard to get into your dream college, or a nursing student studying for a complex exam, we want to help give you the tools you need to succeed. We hope this study guide gives you the skills and the confidence to thrive, and we can't thank you enough for allowing us to be part of your journey.

In an effort to continue to improve our products, we welcome feedback from our customers. We look forward to hearing from you. Suggestions, success stories, and criticisms can all be communicated by emailing us at info@studyguideteam.com.

Sincerely,
Test Prep Books Team

FREE Videos/DVD OFFER

Doing well on your exam requires both knowing the test content and understanding how to use that knowledge to do well on the test. We offer completely FREE test taking tip videos. **These videos cover world-class tips that you can use to succeed on your test.**

To get your **FREE videos**, you can use the QR code below or email freevideos@studyguideteam.com with "Free Videos" in the subject line and the following information in the body of the email:

    a. The title of your product
    b. Your product rating on a scale of 1-5, with 5 being the highest
    c. Your feedback about the product

If you have any questions or concerns, please don't hesitate to contact us at info@studyguideteam.com.

Quick Overview

As you draw closer to taking your exam, effective preparation becomes more and more important. Thankfully, you have this study guide to help you get ready. Use this guide to help keep your studying on track and refer to it often.

This study guide contains several key sections that will help you be successful on your exam. The guide contains tips for what you should do the night before and the day of the test. Also included are test-taking tips. Knowing the right information is not always enough. Many well-prepared test takers struggle with exams. These tips will help equip you to accurately read, assess, and answer test questions.

A large part of the guide is devoted to showing you what content to expect on the exam and to helping you better understand that content. In this guide are practice test questions so that you can see how well you have grasped the content. Then, answer explanations are provided so that you can understand why you missed certain questions.

Don't try to cram the night before you take your exam. This is not a wise strategy for a few reasons. First, your retention of the information will be low. Your time would be better used by reviewing information you already know rather than trying to learn a lot of new information. Second, you will likely become stressed as you try to gain a large amount of knowledge in a short amount of time. Third, you will be depriving yourself of sleep. So be sure to go to bed at a reasonable time the night before. Being well-rested helps you focus and remain calm.

Be sure to eat a substantial breakfast the morning of the exam. If you are taking the exam in the afternoon, be sure to have a good lunch as well. Being hungry is distracting and can make it difficult to focus. You have hopefully spent lots of time preparing for the exam. Don't let an empty stomach get in the way of success!

When travelling to the testing center, leave earlier than needed. That way, you have a buffer in case you experience any delays. This will help you remain calm and will keep you from missing your appointment time at the testing center.

Be sure to pace yourself during the exam. Don't try to rush through the exam. There is no need to risk performing poorly on the exam just so you can leave the testing center early. Allow yourself to use all of the allotted time if needed.

Remain positive while taking the exam even if you feel like you are performing poorly. Thinking about the content you should have mastered will not help you perform better on the exam.

Once the exam is complete, take some time to relax. Even if you feel that you need to take the exam again, you will be well served by some down time before you begin studying again. It's often easier to convince yourself to study if you know that it will come with a reward!

Test-Taking Strategies

1. Predicting the Answer

When you feel confident in your preparation for a multiple-choice test, try predicting the answer before reading the answer choices. This is especially useful on questions that test objective factual knowledge. By predicting the answer before reading the available choices, you eliminate the possibility that you will be distracted or led astray by an incorrect answer choice. You will feel more confident in your selection if you read the question, predict the answer, and then find your prediction among the answer choices. After using this strategy, be sure to still read all of the answer choices carefully and completely. If you feel unprepared, you should not attempt to predict the answers. This would be a waste of time and an opportunity for your mind to wander in the wrong direction.

2. Reading the Whole Question

Too often, test takers scan a multiple-choice question, recognize a few familiar words, and immediately jump to the answer choices. Test authors are aware of this common impatience, and they will sometimes prey upon it. For instance, a test author might subtly turn the question into a negative, or he or she might redirect the focus of the question right at the end. The only way to avoid falling into these traps is to read the entirety of the question carefully before reading the answer choices.

3. Looking for Wrong Answers

Long and complicated multiple-choice questions can be intimidating. One way to simplify a difficult multiple-choice question is to eliminate all of the answer choices that are clearly wrong. In most sets of answers, there will be at least one selection that can be dismissed right away. If the test is administered on paper, the test taker could draw a line through it to indicate that it may be ignored; otherwise, the test taker will have to perform this operation mentally or on scratch paper. In either case, once the obviously incorrect answers have been eliminated, the remaining choices may be considered. Sometimes identifying the clearly wrong answers will give the test taker some information about the correct answer. For instance, if one of the remaining answer choices is a direct opposite of one of the eliminated answer choices, it may well be the correct answer. The opposite of obviously wrong is obviously right! Of course, this is not always the case. Some answers are obviously incorrect simply because they are irrelevant to the question being asked. Still, identifying and eliminating some incorrect answer choices is a good way to simplify a multiple-choice question.

4. Don't Overanalyze

Anxious test takers often overanalyze questions. When you are nervous, your brain will often run wild, causing you to make associations and discover clues that don't actually exist. If you feel that this may be a problem for you, do whatever you can to slow down during the test. Try taking a deep breath or counting to ten. As you read and consider the question, restrict yourself to the particular words used by the author. Avoid thought tangents about what the author *really* meant, or what he or she was *trying* to say. The only things that matter on a multiple-choice test are the words that are actually in the question. You must avoid reading too much into a multiple-choice question, or supposing that the writer meant

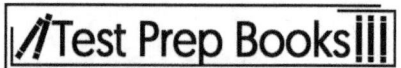

Test-Taking Strategies

something other than what he or she wrote.

5. No Need for Panic

It is wise to learn as many strategies as possible before taking a multiple-choice test, but it is likely that you will come across a few questions for which you simply don't know the answer. In this situation, avoid panicking. Because most multiple-choice tests include dozens of questions, the relative value of a single wrong answer is small. As much as possible, you should compartmentalize each question on a multiple-choice test. In other words, you should not allow your feelings about one question to affect your success on the others. When you find a question that you either don't understand or don't know how to answer, just take a deep breath and do your best. Read the entire question slowly and carefully. Try rephrasing the question a couple of different ways. Then, read all of the answer choices carefully. After eliminating obviously wrong answers, make a selection and move on to the next question.

6. Confusing Answer Choices

When working on a difficult multiple-choice question, there may be a tendency to focus on the answer choices that are the easiest to understand. Many people, whether consciously or not, gravitate to the answer choices that require the least concentration, knowledge, and memory. This is a mistake. When you come across an answer choice that is confusing, you should give it extra attention. A question might be confusing because you do not know the subject matter to which it refers. If this is the case, don't

eliminate the answer before you have affirmatively settled on another. When you come across an answer choice of this type, set it aside as you look at the remaining choices. If you can confidently assert that one of the other choices is correct, you can leave the confusing answer aside. Otherwise, you will need to take a moment to try to better understand the confusing answer choice. Rephrasing is one way to tease out the sense of a confusing answer choice.

7. Your First Instinct

Many people struggle with multiple-choice tests because they overthink the questions. If you have studied sufficiently for the test, you should be prepared to trust your first instinct once you have carefully and completely read the question and all of the answer choices. There is a great deal of research suggesting that the mind can come to the correct conclusion very quickly once it has obtained all of the relevant information. At times, it may seem to you as if your intuition is working faster even than your reasoning mind. This may in fact be true. The knowledge you obtain while studying may be retrieved from your subconscious before you have a chance to work out the associations that support it. Verify your instinct by working out the reasons that it should be trusted.

8. Key Words

Many test takers struggle with multiple-choice questions because they have poor reading comprehension skills. Quickly reading and understanding a multiple-choice question requires a mixture of skill and experience. To help with this, try jotting down a few key words and phrases on a piece of scrap paper. Doing this concentrates the process of reading and forces the mind to weigh the relative importance of the question's parts. In selecting words and phrases to write down, the test taker thinks about the question more deeply and carefully. This is especially true for multiple-choice questions that are preceded by a long prompt.

9. Subtle Negatives

One of the oldest tricks in the multiple-choice test writer's book is to subtly reverse the meaning of a question with a word like *not* or *except*. If you are not paying attention to each word in the question, you can easily be led astray by this trick. For instance, a common question format is, "Which of the following is...?" Obviously, if the question instead is, "Which of the following is not...?," then the answer will be quite different. Even worse, the test makers are aware of the potential for this mistake and will include one answer choice that would be correct if the question were not negated or reversed. A test taker who misses the reversal will find what he or she believes to be a correct answer and will be so confident that he or she will fail to reread the question and discover the original error. The only way to avoid this is to practice a wide variety of multiple-choice questions and to pay close attention to each and every word.

10. Reading Every Answer Choice

It may seem obvious, but you should always read every one of the answer choices! Too many test takers fall into the habit of scanning the question and assuming that they understand the question because they recognize a few key words. From there, they pick the first answer choice that answers the question they believe they have read. Test takers who read all of the answer choices might discover that one of the latter answer choices is actually *more* correct. Moreover, reading all of the answer choices can remind you of facts related to the question that can help you arrive at the correct answer. Sometimes, a misstatement or incorrect detail in one of the latter answer choices will trigger your memory of the subject and will enable you to find the right answer. Failing to read all of the answer choices is like not reading all of the items on a restaurant menu: you might miss out on the perfect choice.

11. Spot the Hedges

One of the keys to success on multiple-choice tests is paying close attention to every word. This is never truer than with words like *almost*, *most*, *some*, and *sometimes*. These words are called "hedges" because they indicate that a statement is not totally true or not true in every place and time. An absolute statement will contain no hedges, but in many subjects, the answers are not always straightforward or absolute. There are always exceptions to the rules in these subjects. For this reason,

you should favor those multiple-choice questions that contain hedging language. The presence of qualifying words indicates that the author is taking special care with his or her words, which is certainly important when composing the right answer. After all, there are many ways to be wrong, but there is only one way to be right! For this reason, it is wise to avoid answers that are absolute when taking a multiple-choice test. An absolute answer is one that says things are either all one way or all another. They often include words like *every*, *always*, *best*, and *never*. If you are taking a multiple-choice test in a subject that doesn't lend itself to absolute answers, be on your guard if you see any of these words.

12. Long Answers

In many subject areas, the answers are not simple. As already mentioned, the right answer often requires hedges. Another common feature of the answers to a complex or subjective question are qualifying clauses, which are groups of words that subtly modify the meaning of the sentence. If the question or answer choice describes a rule to which there are exceptions or the subject matter is complicated, ambiguous, or confusing, the correct answer will require many words in order to be expressed clearly and accurately. In essence, you should not be deterred by answer choices that seem excessively long. Oftentimes, the author of the text will not be able to write the correct answer without offering some qualifications and modifications. Your job is to read the answer choices thoroughly and completely and to select the one that most accurately and precisely answers the question.

13. Restating to Understand

Sometimes, a question on a multiple-choice test is difficult not because of what it asks but because of how it is written. If this is the case, restate the question or answer choice in different words. This process serves a couple of important purposes. First, it forces you to concentrate on the core of the question. In order to rephrase the question accurately, you have to understand it well. Rephrasing the question will concentrate your mind on the key words and ideas. Second, it will present the information to your mind in a fresh way. This process may trigger your memory and render some useful scrap of information picked up while studying.

14. True Statements

Sometimes an answer choice will be true in itself, but it does not answer the question. This is one of the main reasons why it is essential to read the question carefully and completely before proceeding to the answer choices. Too often, test takers skip ahead to the answer choices and look for true statements. Having found one of these, they are content to select it without reference to the question above. The savvy test taker will always read the entire question before turning to the answer choices. Then, having settled on a correct answer choice, he or she will refer to the original question and ensure that the selected answer is relevant. The mistake of choosing a correct-but-irrelevant answer choice is especially common on questions related to specific pieces of objective knowledge.

15. No Patterns

One of the more dangerous ideas that circulates about multiple-choice tests is that the correct answers tend to fall into patterns. These erroneous ideas range from a belief that B and C are the most common right answers, to the idea that an unprepared test-taker should answer "A-B-A-C-A-D-A-B-A." It cannot be emphasized enough that pattern-seeking of this type is exactly the WRONG way to approach a multiple-choice test. To begin with, it is highly unlikely that the test maker will plot the correct answers according to some predetermined pattern. The questions are scrambled and delivered in a random order. Furthermore, even if the test maker was following a pattern in the assignation of correct answers, there is no reason why the test taker would know which pattern he or she was using. Any attempt to discern a pattern in the answer choices is a waste of time and a distraction from the real work of taking the test. A test taker would be much better served by extra preparation before the test than by reliance on a pattern in the answers.

Introduction to the GMAT Focus Edition

Function of the Test

The Graduate Management Admission Test (GMAT) Focus Edition, administered by the Graduate Management Admissions Council (GMAC), is the standard business school admissions exam in the United States. More than 2,100 business schools use the GMAT Focus Edition as part of their admissions criteria for MBA programs as well as other business-related programs like accounting and finance. The test is also used in admissions offices at some business schools around the world. The GMAT Focus Edition is not the only business school admissions test—an increasing number of schools accept GRE scores also or instead—but it remains the most common in the United States.

Approximately 300,000 people take the GMAT Focus Edition every year, although that total varies with the economy and other factors. Although business school admissions departments do consider a variety of factors in making decisions about prospective students, the GMAT Focus Edition score is typically the primary consideration and the most commonly discussed factor.

Test Administration

The GMAT Focus Edition is offered at approximately 600 testing centers in over 100 countries. It is offered year-round, and prospective test takers should either register for the GMAT Focus Edition at mba.com or make an appointment at a time that the test is offered at their preferred location. Upon completion of the exam, test takers can expect to receive their official score reports within 3-5 days. Then, after receiving their scores, test takers can choose to send a free score report to up to five schools.

Each section of the GMAT Focus Edition is made up of computer adaptive tests (CATs), meaning that they are given by computer and that the difficulty of questions offered to the test taker adapts to the test taker's performance up to that point. A unique feature of the GMAT Focus Edition is that test takers can review and edit the answers to the questions in each section before moving on. They will have the opportunity to do this from the Question Review & Edit screen, which appears at the end of each section. Test takers may review as many questions as they would like, but they may only edit up to three answers. Test takers can also bookmark questions as they move throughout the test, allowing an easy return to them from the Question Review & Edit screen.

Individuals are allowed to retake the GMAT Focus Edition as often as they wish, but not more than five times in one twelve-month period, or more than eight times in their life. Reasonable accommodations are available for test takers with disabilities in keeping with the Americans with Disabilities Act.

Test Format

The GMAT Focus Edition is 2 hours and 15 minutes long and includes 64 questions across three sections. There is also an optional 10-minute break. The three sections of the GMAT Focus Edition are Quantitative Reasoning, Verbal Reasoning, and Data Insights. Test takers may complete the test in any section order, and they may take the optional break after any section.

The Quantitative Reasoning section contains twenty-one problem solving questions covering arithmetic and algebra. You cannot use a calculator for this section. The Verbal Reasoning section is intended to

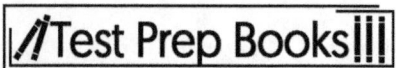

Introduction to the GMAT Focus Edition

measure the test taker's reading comprehension, critical thinking, and problem-solving skills. It contains twenty-three Reading Comprehension and Critical Reasoning questions. The Data Insights section of the GMAT Focus Edition tests for data literacy skills, including the test takers' ability to analyze data and apply it to real-life situations. It contains twenty questions that require test takers to use their data analysis, verbal reasoning, and math skills to solve. There will be an on-screen calculator provided for this section.

A summary of the sections of the GMAT Focus Edition is as follows:

Section	Questions	Time
Quantitative Reasoning	21 questions	45 minutes
Verbal Reasoning	23 questions	45 minutes
Data Insights	20 questions	45 minutes

Scoring

The GMAT Focus Edition score that test takers can choose to report to schools is a scaled score ranging from 205 to 805 reflecting the test taker's combined performance on all three sections of the exam. The average score of all test takers is usually around 540, and the standard deviation of all scores is 90 points, meaning that just over two-thirds of test takers fall in a range from 450 to 630. Top schools such as Harvard and Stanford admit students with average scores of around 700.

GMAT Focus Edition scores are based on the number of correct answers, with no penalty for guessing other than the missed opportunity to provide another correct response.

Study Prep Plan for the GMAT Focus Edition

1 **Schedule** - Use one of our study schedules below or come up with one of your own.

2 **Relax** - Test anxiety can hurt even the best students. There are many ways to reduce stress. Find the one that works best for you.

3 **Execute** - Once you have a good plan in place, be sure to stick to it.

One Week Study Schedule

Day	Topic
Day 1	Quantitative Reasoning
Day 2	Verbal Reasoning
Day 3	Data Insights
Day 4	Practice Test #1
Day 5	Answer Explanations #1
Day 6	Practice Test #2
Day 7	Take Your Exam!

Two Week Study Schedule

Day	Topic	Day	Topic
Day 1	Quantitative Reasoning	Day 8	Recognizing Relationships in the Information
Day 2	Algebra	Day 9	Multi-Source Reasoning
Day 3	Problem Solving	Day 10	Practice Test #1
Day 4	Verbal Reasoning	Day 11	Answer Explanations #1
Day 5	Main Ideas and Supporting Details	Day 12	Practice Test #2
Day 6	Critical Reasoning	Day 13	Answer Explanations #2
Day 7	Data Insights	Day 14	Take Your Exam!

Build your own prep plan by visiting:

testprepbooks.com/prep

Quantitative Reasoning

Arithmetic and Algebra

Arithmetic

Addition with Whole Numbers and Fractions

Addition combines two quantities together. With whole numbers, this is taking two sets of things and merging them into one, then counting the result. For example, $4 + 3 = 7$. When adding numbers, the order does not matter: $3 + 4 = 7$, also. Longer lists of whole numbers can also be added together. The result of adding numbers is called the **sum**.

With fractions, the number on top is the **numerator**, and the number on the bottom is the **denominator**. To add fractions, the denominator must be the same—a **common denominator**. To find a common denominator, the existing numbers on the bottom must be considered, and the lowest number they will both multiply into must be determined. Consider the following equation:

$$\frac{1}{3} + \frac{5}{6} = ?$$

The numbers 3 and 6 both multiply into 6. Three can be multiplied by 2, and 6 can be multiplied by 1. The top and bottom of each fraction must be multiplied by the same number. Then, the numerators are added together to get a new numerator. The following equation is the result:

$$\frac{1}{3} + \frac{5}{6} = \frac{2}{6} + \frac{5}{6} = \frac{7}{6}$$

Subtraction with Whole Numbers and Fractions

Subtraction is taking one quantity away from another, so it is the opposite of addition. The expression $4 - 3$ means taking 3 away from 4. So, $4 - 3 = 1$. In this case, the order matters, since it entails taking one quantity away from the other, rather than just putting two quantities together. The result of subtraction is also called the **difference**.

To subtract fractions, the denominator must be the same. Then, subtract the numerators together to get a new numerator. Here is an example:

$$\frac{1}{3} - \frac{5}{6} = \frac{2}{6} - \frac{5}{6} = \frac{-3}{6} = -\frac{1}{2}$$

Multiplication with Whole Numbers and Fractions

Multiplication is a kind of repeated addition. The expression 4×5 is taking four sets, each of them having five things in them, and putting them all together. That means:

$$4 \times 5 = 5 + 5 + 5 + 5 = 20$$

As with addition, the order of the numbers does not matter. The result of a multiplication problem is called the **product**.

To multiply fractions, the numerators are multiplied to get the new numerator, and the denominators are multiplied to get the new denominator:

$$\frac{1}{3} \times \frac{5}{6} = \frac{1 \times 5}{3 \times 6} = \frac{5}{18}$$

When multiplying fractions, common factors can **cancel** or **divide into one another**, when factors that appear in the numerator of one fraction and the denominator of the other fraction. Here is an example:

$$\frac{1}{3} \times \frac{9}{8} = \frac{1}{1} \times \frac{3}{8}$$

$$1 \times \frac{3}{8} = \frac{3}{8}$$

The numbers 3 and 9 have a common factor of 3, so that factor can be divided out.

Division with Whole Numbers and Fractions

Division is the opposite of multiplication. With whole numbers, it means splitting up one number into sets of equal size. For example, $16 \div 8$ is the number of sets of eight things that can be made out of sixteen things. Thus, $16 \div 8 = 2$. As with subtraction, the order of the numbers will make a difference, here. The answer to a division problem is called the **quotient**, while the number in front of the division sign is called the **dividend**, and the number behind the division sign is called the **divisor**.

To divide fractions, the first fraction must be multiplied with the reciprocal of the second fraction. The **reciprocal** of the fraction $\frac{x}{y}$ is the fraction $\frac{y}{x}$. Here is an example:

$$\frac{1}{3} \div \frac{5}{6} = \frac{1}{3} \times \frac{6}{5} = \frac{6}{15} = \frac{2}{5}$$

Recognizing Equivalent Fractions and Mixed Numbers

The value of a fraction does not change if multiplying or dividing both the numerator and the denominator by the same number (other than 0). In other words, $\frac{x}{y} = \frac{a \times x}{a \times y} = \frac{x \div a}{y \div a}$, as long as a is not 0. This means that $\frac{2}{5} = \frac{4}{10}$, for example. If x and y are integers that have no common factors, then the fraction is said to be **simplified**. This means $\frac{2}{5}$ is simplified, but $\frac{4}{10}$ is not.

Often when working with fractions, the fractions need to be rewritten so that they all share a single denominator—this is called finding a **common denominator** for the fractions. Using two fractions, $\frac{a}{b}$ and $\frac{c}{d}$, the numerator and denominator of the left fraction can be multiplied by d, while the numerator and denominator of the right fraction can be multiplied by b. This provides the fractions $\frac{a \times d}{b \times d}$ and $\frac{c \times b}{d \times b}$ with the common denominator $b \times d$.

A fraction whose numerator is smaller than its denominator is called a **proper fraction**. A fraction whose numerator is bigger than its denominator is called an **improper fraction**. These numbers can be rewritten as a combination of integers and fractions, called a **mixed number**. For example:

$$\frac{6}{5} = \frac{5}{5} + \frac{1}{5} = 1 + \frac{1}{5} \text{ which can be written as: } 1\frac{1}{5}$$

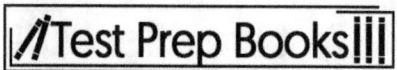

Quantitative Reasoning

Estimating

Estimation is finding a value that is close to a solution but is not the exact answer. For example, if there are values in the thousands to be multiplied, then each value can be estimated to the nearest thousand and the calculation performed. This value provides an approximate solution that can be determined very quickly.

Recognition of Decimals

The **decimal system** is a way of writing out numbers that uses ten different numerals: 0, 1, 2, 3, 4, 5, 6, 7, 8, and 9. This is also called a "base ten" or "base 10" system. Other bases are also used. For example, computers work with a base of 2. This means they only use the numerals 0 and 1.

The **decimal place** denotes how far to the right of the decimal point a numeral is. The first digit to the right of the decimal point is in the *tenths* place. The next is the *hundredths*. The third is the *thousandths*.

So, 3.142 has a 1 in the tenths place, a 4 in the hundredths place, and a 2 in the thousandths place.

The **decimal point** is a period used to separate the *ones* place from the *tenths* place when writing out a number as a decimal.

A **decimal number** is a number written out with a decimal point instead of as a fraction, for example, 1.25 instead of $\frac{5}{4}$. Depending on the situation, it can sometimes be easier to work with fractions and sometimes easier to work with decimal numbers.

A decimal number is **terminating** if it stops at some point. It is called **repeating** if it never stops but repeats over and over. It is important to note that every rational number can be written as a terminating decimal or as a repeating decimal.

Addition with Decimals

To add decimal numbers, each number in the columns needs to be lined up by the decimal point. For each number being added, the zeros to the right of the last number need to be filled in so that each of the numbers has the same number of places to the right of the decimal. Then, the columns can be added together. Here is an example of $2.45 + 1.3 + 8.891$ written in column form:

$$\begin{array}{r} 2.450 \\ 1.300 \\ + 8.891 \end{array}$$

Zeros have been added in the columns so that each number has the same number of places to the right of the decimal.

Added together, the correct answer is 12.641:

$$\begin{array}{r} 2.450 \\ 1.300 \\ + 8.891 \\ \hline 12.641 \end{array}$$

Quantitative Reasoning

Subtraction with Decimals
Subtracting decimal numbers is the same process as adding decimals. Here is 7.89 − 4.235 written in column form:

$$\begin{array}{r} 7.890 \\ -\,4.235 \\ \hline 3.655 \end{array}$$

A zero has been added in the column so that each number has the same number of places to the right of the decimal.

Multiplication with Decimals
The simplest way to multiply decimals is to calculate the product as if the decimals are not there, then count the number of decimal places in the original problem. Use that total to place the decimal the same number of places over in your answer, counting from right to left. For example, 0.5×1.25 can be rewritten and multiplied as 5×125, which equals 625. Then the decimal is added three places from the right for .625.

The final answer will have the same number of decimal points as the total number of decimal places in the problem. The first number has one decimal place, and the second number has two decimal places. Therefore, the final answer will contain three decimal places:

$$0.5 \times 1.25 = 0.625$$

Division with Decimals
Dividing a decimal by a whole number entails using long division first by ignoring the decimal point. Then, the decimal point is moved the number of places given in the problem.

For example, $6.8 \div 4$ can be rewritten as $68 \div 4$, which is 17. There is one non-zero integer to the right of the decimal point, so the final solution would have one decimal place to the right of the solution. In this case, the solution is 1.7.

Dividing a decimal by another decimal requires changing the divisor to a whole number by moving its decimal point. The decimal place of the dividend should be moved by the same number of places as the divisor. Then, the problem is the same as dividing a decimal by a whole number.

For example, $5.72 \div 1.1$ has a divisor with one decimal point in the denominator. The expression can be rewritten as $57.2 \div 11$ by moving each number one decimal place to the right to eliminate the decimal. The long division can be completed as $572 \div 11$ with a result of 52. Since there is one non-zero integer to the right of the decimal point in the problem, the final solution is 5.2.

In another example, $8 \div 0.16$ has a divisor with two decimal points in the denominator. The expression can be rewritten as $800 \div 16$ by moving each number two decimal places to the right to eliminate the decimal in the divisor. The long division can be completed with a result of 50.

Fraction and Percent Equivalencies
The word **percent** comes from the Latin phrase for "per one hundred." A percent is a way of writing out a fraction. It is a fraction with a denominator of 100. Thus, $65\% = \frac{65}{100}$.

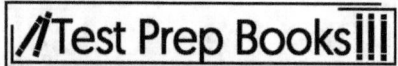

Quantitative Reasoning

To convert a fraction to a percent, the denominator is written as 100. For example:

$$\frac{3}{5} = \frac{60}{100} = 60\%$$

In converting a percent to a fraction, the percent is written with a denominator of 100, and the result is simplified. For example:

$$30\% = \frac{30}{100} = \frac{3}{10}$$

Percent Problems

The basic percent equation is the following:

$$\frac{is}{of} = \frac{\%}{100}$$

The placement of numbers in the equation depends on what the question asks.

Example 1

Find 40% of 80.

Basically, the problem is asking, "What is 40% of 80?" The 40% is the percent, and 80 is the number to find the percent "of." The equation is:

$$\frac{x}{80} = \frac{40}{100}$$

Solving the equation by cross-multiplication, the problem becomes $100x = 80(40)$. Solving for x produces the answer: $x = 32$.

Example 2

What percent of 100 is 20?

20 fills in the "is" portion, while 100 fills in the "of." The question asks for the percent, so that will be x, the unknown. The following equation is set up:

$$\frac{20}{100} = \frac{x}{100}$$

Cross-multiplying yields the equation $100x = 20(100)$. Solving for x gives the answer: 20%.

Example 3

30% of what number is 30?

The following equation uses the clues and numbers in the problem:

$$\frac{30}{x} = \frac{30}{100}$$

Quantitative Reasoning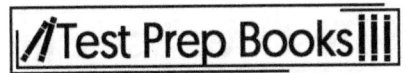

Cross-multiplying results in the equation $30(100) = 30x$. Solving for x gives the answer: $x = 100$.

Problems Involving Estimation
Sometimes when multiplying numbers, the result can be estimated by **rounding**. For example, to estimate the value of 11.2×2.01, each number can be rounded to the nearest integer. This will yield a result of 22.

Rate, Percent, and Measurement Problems
A **ratio** compares the size of one group to the size of another. For example, there may be a room with 4 tables and 24 chairs. The ratio of tables to chairs is 4: 24. Such ratios behave like fractions in that both sides of the ratio by the same number can be multiplied or divided. Thus, the ratio 4:24 is the same as the ratio 2:12 and 1:6.

One quantity is **proportional** to another quantity if the first quantity is always some multiple of the second. For instance, the distance travelled in five hours is always five times to the speed as travelled. The distance is proportional to speed in this case.

One quantity is **inversely proportional** to another quantity if the first quantity is equal to some number divided by the second quantity. The time it takes to travel one hundred miles will be given by 100 divided by the speed travelled. The time is inversely proportional to the speed.

When dealing with word problems, there is no fixed series of steps to follow, but there are some general guidelines to use. It is important that the quantity to be found is identified. Then, it can be determined how the given values can be used and manipulated to find the final answer.

Example 1

Jana wants to travel to visit Alice, who lives one hundred and fifty miles away. If she can drive at fifty miles per hour, how long will her trip take?

The quantity to find is the *time* of the trip. The time of a trip is given by the distance to travel divided by the speed to be traveled. The problem determines that the distance is one hundred and fifty miles, while the speed is fifty miles per hour. Thus, 150 divided by 50 is $150 \div 50 = 3$. Because *miles* and *miles per hour* are the units being divided, the miles cancel out. The result is 3 hours.

Example 2

Bernard wishes to paint a wall that measures twenty feet wide by eight feet high. It costs ten cents to paint one square foot. How much money will Bernard need for paint?

The final quantity to compute is the *cost* to paint the wall. This will be ten cents ($0.10) for each square foot of area needed to paint. The area to be painted is unknown, but the dimensions of the wall are given; thus, it can be calculated.

The dimensions of the wall are 20 feet wide and 8 feet high. Since the area of a rectangle is length multiplied by width, the area of the wall is $8 \times 20 = 160$ square feet. Multiplying 0.1×160 yields $16 as the cost of the paint.

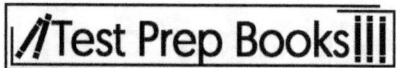

The **average** or **mean** of a collection of numbers is given by adding those numbers together and then dividing by the total number of values. A **weighted average** or **weighted mean** is given by adding the numbers multiplied by their weights, then dividing by the sum of the weights:

$$\frac{w_1 x_1 + w_2 x_2 + w_3 x_3 \ldots + w_n x_n}{w_1 + w_2 + w_3 + \ldots + w_n}$$

An **ordinary average** is a weighted average where all the weights are 1.

Distribution of a Quantity into its Fractional Parts

A quantity may be broken into its fractional parts. For example, a toy box holds three types of toys for kids. $\frac{1}{3}$ of the toys are Type A and $\frac{1}{4}$ of the toys are Type B. With that information, how many Type C toys are there?

First, the sum of Type A and Type B must be determined by finding a common denominator to add the fractions. The lowest common multiple is 12, so that is what will be used. The sum is:

$$\frac{1}{3} + \frac{1}{4} = \frac{4}{12} + \frac{3}{12} = \frac{7}{12}$$

This value is subtracted from 1 to find the number of Type C toys. The value is subtracted from 1 because 1 represents a whole. The calculation is:

$$1 - \frac{7}{12} = \frac{12}{12} - \frac{7}{12} = \frac{5}{12}$$

This means that $\frac{5}{12}$ of the toys are Type C. To check the answer, add all fractions together, and the result should be 1.

Algebra

Solving for X in Proportions

Proportions are commonly used to solve word problems to find unknown values such as x that are some percent or fraction of a known number. Proportions are solved by cross-multiplying and then dividing to arrive at x. The following examples show how this is done:

1) $\frac{75\%}{90\%} = \frac{25\%}{x}$

To solve for x, the fractions must be cross multiplied:

$$75\% x = 90\% \times 25\%$$

To make things easier, let's convert the percentages to decimals:

$$0.9 \times 0.25 = 0.225 = 0.75x$$

To get rid of x's coefficient, each side must be divided by that same coefficient to get the answer $x = 0.3$. The question could ask for the answer as a percentage or fraction in lowest terms, which are 30% and $\frac{3}{10}$, respectively.

Quantitative Reasoning

2) $\frac{x}{12} = \frac{30}{96}$

Cross-multiply: $96x = 30 \times 12$
Multiply: $96x = 360$
Divide: $x = 360 \div 96$
Answer: $x = 3.75$

3) $\frac{0.5}{3} = \frac{x}{6}$

Cross-multiply: $3x = 0.5 \times 6$
Multiply: $3x = 3$
Divide: $x = 3 \div 3$
Answer: $x = 1$

You may have noticed there's a faster way to arrive at the answer. If there is an obvious operation being performed on the proportion, the same operation can be used on the other side of the proportion to solve for x. For example, in the first practice problem, 75% became 25% when divided by 3, and upon doing the same to 90%, the correct answer of 30% would have been found with much less legwork. However, these questions aren't always so intuitive, so it's a good idea to work through the steps, even if the answer seems apparent from the outset.

Translating Words into Math

To translate a word problem into an expression, look for a series of key words indicating addition, subtraction, multiplication, or division:

Addition: *add, altogether, together, plus, increased by, more than, in all, sum,* and *total*

Subtraction: *minus, less than, difference, decreased by, fewer than, remain,* and *take away*

Multiplication: *times, twice, of, double,* and *triple*

Division: *divided by, cut up, half, quotient of, split,* and *shared equally*

If a question asks to give words to a mathematical expression and says "equals," then an = sign must be included in the answer. Similarly, "less than or equal to" is expressed by the inequality symbol ≤, and "greater than or equal" to is expressed as ≥. Furthermore, "less than" is represented by <, and "greater than" is expressed by >.

Word Problems

Word problems can appear daunting, but don't let the verbiage psych you out. No matter the scenario or specifics, the key to answering them is to translate the words into a math problem. Always keep in mind what the question is asking and what operations could lead to that answer. The following word problem resembles one of the question types most frequently encountered on the exam.

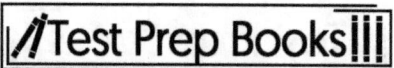

Quantitative Reasoning

Working with Money

Walter's Coffee Shop sells a variety of drinks and breakfast treats.

Price List	
Hot Coffee	$2.00
Slow-Drip Iced Coffee	$3.00
Latte	$4.00
Muffin	$2.00
Crepe	$4.00
Egg Sandwich	$5.00

Costs	
Hot Coffee	$0.25
Slow-Drip Iced Coffee	$0.75
Latte	$1.00
Muffin	$1.00
Crepe	$2.00
Egg Sandwich	$3.00

Walter's utilities, rent, and labor costs him $500 per day. Today, Walter sold 200 hot coffees, 100 slow-drip iced coffees, 50 lattes, 75 muffins, 45 crepes, and 60 egg sandwiches. What was Walter's total profit today?

To accurately answer this type of question, determine the total cost of making his drinks and treats, then determine how much revenue he earned from selling those products. After arriving at these two totals, the profit is measured by deducting the total cost from the total revenue.

Walter's costs for today:

Item	Quantity	Cost Per Unit	Total Cost
Hot Coffee	200	$0.25	$50
Slow-Drip Iced Coffee	100	$0.75	$75
Latte	50	$1.00	$50
Muffin	75	$1.00	$75
Crepe	45	$2.00	$90
Egg Sandwich	60	$3.00	$180
Utilities, rent, and labor			$500
Total Costs			$1,020

Quantitative Reasoning

Walter's revenue for today:

Item	Quantity	Revenue Per Unit	Total Revenue
Hot Coffee	200	$2.00	$400
Slow-Drip Iced Coffee	100	$3.00	$300
Latte	50	$4.00	$200
Muffin	75	$2.00	$150
Crepe	45	$4.00	$180
Egg Sandwich	60	$5.00	$300
Total Revenue			$1,530

$$\text{Walter's Profit} = \text{Revenue} - \text{Costs} = \$1,530 - \$1,020 = \$510$$

This strategy is applicable to other question types. For example, calculating salary after deductions, balancing a checkbook, and calculating a dinner bill are common word problems similar to business planning. Just remember to use the correct operations. When a balance is increased, use addition. When a balance is decreased, use subtraction. Common sense and organization are your greatest assets when answering word problems.

Unit Rate

Unit rate word problems will ask to calculate the rate or quantity of something in a different value. For example, a problem might say that a car drove a certain number of miles in a certain number of minutes and then ask how many miles per hour the car was traveling. These questions involve solving proportions. Consider the following examples:

1) Alexandra made $96 during the first 3 hours of her shift as a temporary worker at a law office. She will continue to earn money at this rate until she finishes in 5 more hours. How much does Alexandra make per hour? How much will Alexandra have made at the end of the day?

This problem can be solved in two ways. The first is to set up a proportion, as the rate of pay is constant. The second is to determine her hourly rate, multiply the 5 hours by that rate, and then add the $96.

To set up a proportion, put the money already earned over the hours already worked on one side of an equation. The other side has x over 8 hours (the total hours worked in the day). It looks like this:

$$\frac{96}{3} = \frac{x}{8}$$

Now, cross-multiply to get $768 = 3x$. To get x, divide by 3, which leaves $x = 256$. Alternatively, as x is the numerator of one of the proportions, multiplying by its denominator will reduce the solution by one step. Thus, Alexandra will make $256 at the end of the day. To calculate her hourly rate, divide the total by 8, giving $32 per hour.

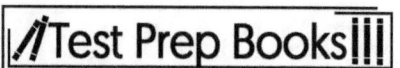

Quantitative Reasoning

Alternatively, it is possible to figure out the hourly rate by dividing $96 by 3 hours to get $32 per hour. Now her total pay can be figured by multiplying $32 per hour by 8 hours, which comes out to $256.

2) Jonathan is reading a novel. So far, he has read 215 of the 335 total pages. It takes Jonathan 25 minutes to read 10 pages, and the rate is constant. How long does it take Jonathan to read one page? How much longer will it take him to finish the novel? Express the answer in time.

To calculate how long it takes Jonathan to read one page, divide the 25 minutes by 10 pages to determine the page per minute rate. Thus, it takes 2.5 minutes to read one page.

Jonathan must read 120 more pages to complete the novel. (This is calculated by subtracting the pages already read from the total.) Now, multiply his rate per page by the number of pages. Thus,

$$120 \times 2.5 = 300$$

Expressed in time, 300 minutes is equal to 5 hours.

3) At a hotel, $\frac{4}{5}$ of the 120 rooms are booked for Saturday. On Sunday, $\frac{3}{4}$ of the rooms are booked. On which day are more of the rooms booked, and by how many more?

The first step is to calculate the number of rooms booked for each day. Do this by multiplying the fraction of the rooms booked by the total number of rooms.

Saturday: $\frac{4}{5} \times 120 = \frac{4}{5} \times \frac{120}{1} = \frac{480}{5} = 96$ rooms

Sunday: $\frac{3}{4} \times 120 = \frac{3}{4} \times \frac{120}{1} = \frac{360}{4} = 90$ rooms

Thus, more rooms were booked on Saturday by 6 rooms.

4) In a veterinary hospital, the veterinarian-to-pet ratio is 1:9. The ratio is always constant. If there are 45 pets in the hospital, how many veterinarians are currently in the veterinary hospital?

Set up a proportion to solve for the number of veterinarians:

$$\frac{1}{9} = \frac{x}{45}$$

Cross-multiplying results in $9x = 45$, which works out to 5 veterinarians.

Alternatively, as there are always 9 times as many pets as veterinarians, it is possible to divide the number of pets (45) by 9. This also arrives at the correct answer of 5 veterinarians.

5) At a general practice law firm, 30% of the lawyers work solely on tort cases. If 9 lawyers work solely on tort cases, how many lawyers work at the firm?

First, solve for the total number of lawyers working at the firm, which will be represented here with x. The problem states that 9 lawyers work solely on torts cases, and they make up 30% of the total lawyers at the firm. Thus, 30% multiplied by the total, x, will equal 9. Written as equation, this is:

$$30\% \times x = 9$$

Quantitative Reasoning

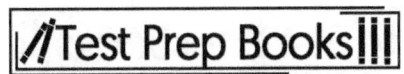

It's easier to deal with the equation after converting the percentage to a decimal, leaving $0.3x = 9$. Thus, $x = \frac{9}{0.3} = 30$ lawyers working at the firm.

6) Xavier was hospitalized with pneumonia. He was originally given 35mg of antibiotics. Later, after his condition continued to worsen, Xavier's dosage was increased to 60mg. What was the percent increase of the antibiotics? Round the percentage to the nearest tenth.

An increase or decrease in percentage can be calculated by dividing the difference in amounts by the original amount and multiplying by 100. Written as an equation, the formula is:

$$\frac{\text{new quantity} - \text{old quantity}}{\text{old quantity}} \times 100$$

Here, the question states that the dosage was increased from 35mg to 60mg, so these are plugged into the formula to find the percentage increase.

$$\frac{60 - 35}{35} \times 100 = \frac{25}{35} \times 100$$

$$0.7142 \times 100 = 71.4\%$$

Order of Rational Numbers

A common question type asks to order rational numbers from least to greatest or greatest to least. The numbers will come in a variety of formats, including decimals, percentages, roots, fractions, and whole numbers. These questions test for knowledge of different types of numbers and the ability to determine their respective values.

Whether the question asks to order the numbers from greatest to least or least to greatest, the crux of the question is the same—convert the numbers into a common format. Generally, it's easiest to write the numbers as whole numbers and decimals so they can be placed on a number line. Follow these examples to understand this strategy.

1) Order the following rational numbers from greatest to least:

$$\sqrt{36}, 0.65, 78\%, \frac{3}{4}, 7, 90\%, \frac{5}{2}$$

Of the seven numbers, the whole number (7) and decimal (0.65) are already in an accessible form, so concentrate on the other five.

First, the square root of 36 equals 6. (If the test asks for the root of a non-perfect root, determine which two whole numbers the root lies between.) Next, convert the percentages to decimals. A percentage means "per hundred," so this conversion requires moving the decimal point two places to the left, leaving 0.78 and 0.9. Lastly, evaluate the fractions:

$$\frac{3}{4} = \frac{75}{100} = 0.75 \; ; \frac{5}{2} = 2\frac{1}{2} = 2.5$$

Now, the only step left is to list the numbers in the request order:

$$7, \sqrt{36}, \frac{5}{2}, 90\%, 78\%, \frac{3}{4}, 0.65$$

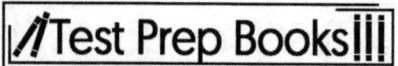

2) Order the following rational numbers from least to greatest:

$$2.5, \sqrt{9}, -10.5, 0.853, 175\%, \sqrt{4}, \frac{4}{5}$$

$$\sqrt{9} = 3$$

$$175\% = 1.75$$

$$\sqrt{4} = 2$$

$$\frac{4}{5} = 0.8$$

From least to greatest, the answer is: -10.5, $\frac{4}{5}$, 0.853, 175%, $\sqrt{4}$, 2.5, $\sqrt{9}$,

FOIL Method

FOIL is a technique for generating polynomials through the multiplication of binomials. A polynomial is an expression of multiple variables (for example, x, y, z) in at least three terms involving only the four basic operations and exponents. FOIL is an acronym for First, Outer, Inner, and Last. "First" represents the multiplication of the terms appearing first in the binomials. "Outer" means multiplying the outermost terms. "Inner" means multiplying the terms inside. "Last" means multiplying the last terms of each binomial.

After completing FOIL and solving the operations, like terms are combined. To identify like terms, look for terms with the same variable and the same exponent. For example, look at:

$$4x^2 - x^2 + 15x + 2x^2 - 8$$

The $4x^2, -x^2$, and $2x^2$ are all like terms because they have the variable (x) and exponent (2). Thus, after combining the like terms, the polynomial has been simplified:

$$5x^2 + 15x - 8$$

The purpose of FOIL is to simplify an equation involving multiple variables and operations. Although it sounds complicated, working through some examples will provide some clarity:

1) Simplify $(x + 10)(x + 4) = (x \times x) + (x \times 4) + (10 \times x) + (10 \times 4)$
                                                                    First   Outer   Inner   Last

After multiplying these binomials, it's time to solve the operations and combine like terms. Thus, the expression becomes:

$$x^2 + 4x + 10x + 40 = x^2 + 14x + 40$$

2) Simplify $2x(4x^3 - 7y^2 + 3x^2 + 4)$

Here, a monomial ($2x$) is multiplied into a polynomial:

$$(4x^3 - 7y^2 + 3x^2 + 4)$$

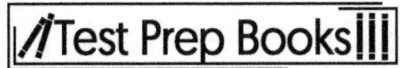

Using the distributive property, multiply the monomial against each term in the polynomial. This becomes:

$$2x(4x^3) - 2x(7y^2) + 2x(3x^2) + 2x(4).$$

Now, simplify each monomial. Start with the coefficients:

$$(2 \times 4)(x \times x^3) - (2 \times 7)(x \times y^2) + (2 \times 3)(x \times x^2) + (2 \times 4)(x)$$

When multiplying powers with the same base, add their exponents. Remember, a variable with no listed exponent has an exponent of 1, and exponents of distinct variables cannot be combined. This produces the answer:

$$8x^{1+3} - 14xy^2 + 6x^{1+2} + 8x = 8x^4 - 14xy^2 + 6x^3 + 8x$$

3) Simplify $(8x^{10}y^2z^4) \div (4x^2y^4z^7)$

First, divide the coefficients of the first two polynomials: $8 \div 4 = 2$. Second, divide exponents with the same variable, which requires subtracting the exponents. This results in:

$$2(x^{10-2}y^{2-4}z^{4-7}) = 2x^8y^{-2}z^{-3}$$

However, the most simplified answer should include only positive exponents. Thus, $y^{-2}z^{-3}$ needs to be converted into fractions, respectively $\frac{1}{y^2}$ and $\frac{1}{z^3}$. Since the $2x^8$ has a positive exponent, it is placed in the numerator, and $\frac{1}{y^2}$ and $\frac{1}{z^3}$ are combined into the denominator, leaving $\frac{2x^8}{y^2z^3}$ as the final answer.

Rational Expressions

A **rational expression** is a fraction where the numerator and denominator are both polynomials. Some examples of rational expressions include the following: $\frac{4x^3y^5}{3z^4}$, $\frac{4x^3+3x}{x^2}$, and $\frac{x^2+7x+10}{x+2}$. Since these refer to expressions and not equations, they can be simplified but not solved. Using the rules in the previous *Exponents* and *Roots* sections, some rational expressions with monomials can be simplified. Other rational expressions such as the last example, $\frac{x^2+7x+10}{x+2}$, require more steps to be simplified. First, the polynomial on top can be factored from $x^2 + 7x + 10$ into $(x + 5)(x + 2)$. Then the common factors can be canceled, and the expression can be simplified to $(x + 5)$.

The following problem is an example of using rational expressions:

Reggie wants to lay sod in his rectangular backyard. The length of the yard is given by the expression $4x + 2$, and the width is unknown. The area of the yard is $20x + 10$. Reggie needs to find the width of the yard. Knowing that the area of a rectangle is length multiplied by width, an expression can be written to find the width: $\frac{20x+10}{4x+2}$, area divided by length. Simplifying this expression by factoring out 10 on the top and 2 on the bottom leads to this expression: $\frac{10(2x+1)}{2(2x+1)}$. Cancelling out the $2x + 1$ results in $\frac{10}{2} = 5$. The width of the yard is found to be 5 by simplifying the rational expression.

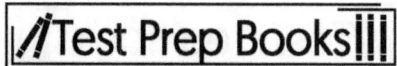

Rational Equations

A **rational equation** can be as simple as an equation with a ratio of polynomials, $\frac{p(x)}{q(x)}$, set equal to a value, where $p(x)$ and $q(x)$ are both polynomials. A rational equation has an equal sign, which is different from expressions. This leads to solutions, or numbers that make the equation true.

It is possible to solve rational equations by trying to get all of the x terms out of the denominator and then isolating them on one side of the equation. For example, to solve the equation $\frac{3x+2}{2x+3} = 4$, both sides get multiplied by $(2x + 3)$. This will cancel on the left side to yield $3x + 2 = 4(2x + 3)$, then:

$$3x + 2 = 8x + 12$$

Now, subtract $8x$ from both sides, which yields:

$$-5x + 2 = 12$$

Subtracting 2 from both sides results in $-5x = 10$. Finally, both sides get divided by -5 to obtain $x = -2$.

Sometimes, when solving rational equations, it can be easier to try to simplify the rational expression by factoring the numerator and denominator first, then cancelling out common factors. For example, to solve $\frac{2x^2-8x+6}{x^2-3x+2} = 1$, the first step is to factor:

$$2x^2 - 8x + 6 = 2(x^2 - 4x + 3)$$

$$2(x - 1)(x - 3)$$

Then, factor $x^2 - 3x + 2$ into $(x - 1)(x - 2)$. This turns the original equation into:

$$\frac{2(x - 1)(x - 3)}{(x - 1)(x - 2)} = 1$$

The common factor of $(x - 1)$ can be canceled, leaving:

$$\frac{2(x - 3)}{x - 2} = 1$$

Now the same method used in the previous example can be followed. Multiplying both sides by $x - 1$ and performing the multiplication on the left yields $2x - 6 = x - 2$, which can be simplified to $x = 4$.

Rational Functions

A **rational function** is similar to an equation, but it includes two variables. In general, a rational function is in the form: $f(x) = \frac{p(x)}{q(x)}$, where $p(x)$ and $q(x)$ are polynomials. Refer to the *Functions* section (which follows) for a more detailed definition of functions. Rational functions are defined everywhere except where the denominator is equal to zero. When the denominator is equal to zero, this indicates either a hole in the graph or an asymptote.

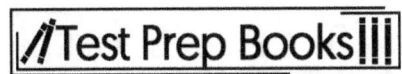

Algebraic Functions

A function is called **algebraic** if it is built up from polynomials by adding, subtracting, multiplying, dividing, and taking radicals. This means that, for example, the variable can never appear in an exponent. Thus, polynomials and rational functions are algebraic, but exponential functions are not algebraic. It turns out that logarithms and trigonometric functions are not algebraic either.

A function of the form $f(x) = a_n x^n + a_{n-1} x^{n-1} + a_{n-2} x^{n-2} + \ldots + a_1 x + a_0$ is called a **polynomial function**. The value of n is called the **degree** of the polynomial. In the case where $n = 1$, it is called a **linear function**. In the case where $n = 2$, it is called a **quadratic function**. In the case where $n = 3$, it is called a **cubic function**.

When n is even, the polynomial is called **even**, and not all real numbers will be in its range. When n is odd, the polynomial is called **odd**, and the range includes all real numbers.

The graph of a quadratic function $f(x) = ax^2 + bx + c$ will be a **parabola**. To see whether or not the parabola opens up or down, it's necessary to check the coefficient of x^2, which is the value a. If the coefficient is positive, then the parabola opens upward. If the coefficient is negative, then the parabola opens downward.

The quantity $D = b^2 - 4ac$ is called the **discriminant** of the parabola. If the discriminant is positive, then the parabola has two real zeros. If the discriminant is negative, then it has no real zeros. If the discriminant is zero, then the parabola's highest or lowest point is on the x-axis, and it has a single real zero.

The highest or lowest point of the parabola is called the **vertex**. The coordinates of the vertex are given by the point $(-\frac{b}{2a}, -\frac{D}{4a})$. The roots of a quadratic function can be found with the quadratic formula, which is:

$$x = \frac{-b \pm \sqrt{b^2 - 4ac}}{2a}$$

A **rational function** is a function $f(x) = \frac{p(x)}{q(x)}$, where p and q are both polynomials. The domain of f will be all real numbers except the (real) roots of q. At these roots, the graph of f will have a **vertical asymptote**, unless they are also roots of p. Here is an example to consider:

$$p(x) = p_n x^n + p_{n-1} x^{n-1} + p_{n-2} x^{n-2} + \ldots + p_1 x + p_0$$

$$q(x) = q_m x^m + q_{m-1} x^{m-1} + q_{m-2} x^{m-2} + \ldots + q_1 x + q_0$$

When the degree of p is less than the degree of q, there will be a **horizontal asymptote** of $y = 0$. If p and q have the same degree, there will be a horizontal asymptote of $y = \frac{p_n}{q_n}$. If the degree of p is exactly one greater than the degree of q, then f will have an oblique asymptote along the line:

$$y = \frac{p_n}{q_{n-1}} x + \frac{p_{n-1}}{q_{n-1}}$$

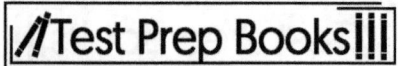

Quantitative Reasoning

Plane Geometry

Locations on the plane that have no width or breadth are called **points**. These points usually will be denoted with capital letters such as *P*.

Any pair of points *A*, *B* on the plane will determine a unique straight line between them. This line is denoted *AB*. Sometimes to emphasize a line is being considered, this will be written as $\overleftrightarrow{AB}$.

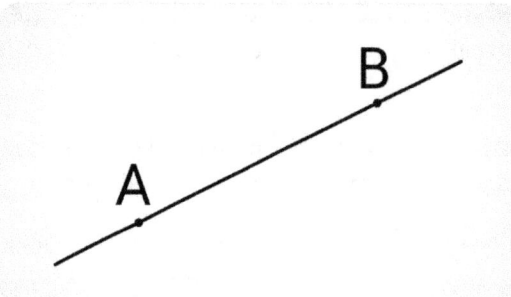

If the Cartesian coordinates for *A* and *B* are known, then the distance $d(A,B)$ along the line between them can be measured using the **Pythagorean formula**, which states that if $A = (x_1, y_1)$ and $B = (x_2, y_2)$, then the distance between them is:

$$d(A, B) = \sqrt{(x_2 - x_1)^2 + (y_2 - y_1)^2}$$

Problem Solving

The Quantitative Reasoning section of the GMAT Focus Edition is made up of 21 problem solving questions that test algebraic and arithmetic foundational knowledge. While the format and objective of each these types of questions are different, the domains of mathematics addressed in either type of question are the same and include the following:

- Arithmetic
- Elementary algebra
- Word Problems

The format of problem solving questions will likely be familiar for most test takers. These present a problem that addresses the basic mathematical skills and concepts listed above and offers five possible answer choices. Test takers must solve the problem and then select the single correct answer choice. The problem-solving questions are designed to be at a difficulty level that is on par with what is expected of an eleventh-grade student. Test takers should expect to demonstrate an understanding of elementary math concepts, reason quantitatively, and apply algebraic and arithmetic knowledge to real-world problems.

Verbal Reasoning

Reading Comprehension

Purpose of a Passage

No matter the genre or format, all authors are writing to persuade, inform, entertain, or express feelings. Often, these purposes are blended, with one dominating the rest. It's useful to learn to recognize the author's intent.

Persuasive writing is used to persuade or convince readers of something. It often contains two elements: the argument and the counterargument. The argument takes a stance on an issue, while the counterargument pokes holes in the opposition's stance. Authors rely on logic, emotion, and writer credibility to persuade readers to agree with them. If readers are opposed to the stance before reading, they are unlikely to adopt that stance. However, those who are undecided or committed to the same stance are more likely to agree with the author.

Informative writing tries to teach or inform. Workplace manuals, instructor lessons, statistical reports, and cookbooks are examples of informative texts. Informative writing is usually based on facts and is often void of emotion and persuasion. Informative texts generally contain statistics, charts, and graphs. Though most informative texts lack a persuasive agenda, readers still must examine the text carefully to determine whether one exists within a given passage.

Stories or narratives are designed to entertain. When you go to the movies, you often want to escape for a few hours, not necessarily to think critically. Entertaining writing is designed to delight and engage the reader. However, sometimes this type of writing can be woven into more serious materials, such as persuasive or informative writing to hook the reader before transitioning into a more scholarly discussion.

Emotional writing works to evoke the reader's feelings, such as anger, euphoria, or sadness. The connection between reader and author is an attempt to cause the reader to share the author's intended emotion or tone. Sometimes in order to make a piece more poignant, the author simply wants readers to feel the same emotions that the author has felt. Other times, the author attempts to persuade or manipulate the reader into adopting his stance. While it's okay to sympathize with the author, be aware of the individual's underlying intent.

Types of Writing Styles

Writing can be classified under four styles: narrative, expository, descriptive (sometimes called technical), and persuasive. Though these types are not mutually exclusive, one form tends to dominate the rest. By recognizing the *type* of passage you're reading, you gain insight into *how* you should read. If you're reading a narrative, you can assume the author intends to entertain, which means you may skim the text without losing meaning. A technical document might require a close read because skimming the passage might cause the reader to miss salient details.

1. **Narrative** writing, at its core, is the art of storytelling. For a narrative to exist, certain elements must be present. First, it must have characters. While many characters are human, characters could be

defined as anything that thinks, acts, and talks like a human. For example, many recent movies, such as *Lord of the Rings* and *The Chronicles of Narnia*, include animals, fantastical creatures, and even trees that behave like humans. Second, it must have a plot or sequence of events. Typically, those events follow a standard plot diagram, but recent trends start *in medias res* or in the middle (near the climax). In this instance, foreshadowing and flashbacks often fill in plot details. Finally, along with characters and a plot, there must also be conflict. Conflict is usually divided into two types: internal and external. Internal conflict indicates the character is in turmoil and is presented through the character's thoughts. External conflicts are visible. Types of external conflict include a person versus nature, another person, or society.

2. **Expository** writing is detached and to the point. Since expository writing is designed to instruct or inform, it usually involves directions and steps written in second person ("you" voice) and lacks any persuasive or narrative elements. Sequence words such as *first*, *second*, and *third*, or *in the first place*, *secondly*, and *lastly* are often given to add fluency and cohesion. Common examples of expository writing include instructor's lessons, cookbook recipes, and repair manuals.

3. Due to its empirical nature, **technical** writing is filled with steps, charts, graphs, data, and statistics. The goal of technical writing is to advance understanding in a field through the scientific method. Experts such as teachers, doctors, or mechanics use words unique to the profession in which they operate. These words, which often incorporate acronyms, are called **jargon**. Technical writing is a type of expository writing but is not meant to be understood by the general public. Instead, technical writers assume readers have received a formal education in a particular field of study and need no explanation as to what the jargon means. Imagine a doctor trying to understand a diagnostic reading for a car or a mechanic trying to interpret lab results. Only professionals with proper training will fully comprehend the text.

4. **Persuasive** writing is designed to change opinions and attitudes. The topic, stance, and arguments are found in the thesis, positioned near the end of the introduction. Later supporting paragraphs offer relevant quotations, paraphrases, and summaries from primary or secondary sources, which are then interpreted, analyzed, and evaluated. The goal of persuasive writers is not to stack quotes but to develop original ideas by using sources as a starting point. Good persuasive writing makes powerful arguments with valid sources and thoughtful analysis. Poor persuasive writing is riddled with bias and logical fallacies. Sometimes logical and illogical arguments are sandwiched together in the same piece. Therefore, readers should display skepticism when reading persuasive arguments.

Text Structure

Depending on what the author is attempting to accomplish, certain formats or text structures work better than others. For example, a sequence structure might work for narration but not for identifying similarities and differences between concepts. Similarly, a comparison-contrast structure is not useful for narration. It's the author's job to put the right information in the correct format.

Readers should be familiar with the five main literary structures:

1. **Sequence** structure (sometimes referred to as the order structure) is when the order of events proceed in a predictable order. In many cases, this means the text goes through the plot elements: exposition, rising action, climax, falling action, and resolution. Readers are introduced to characters, setting, and conflict in the exposition. In the rising action, there's an increase in tension and suspense.

Verbal Reasoning

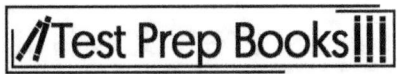

The climax is the height of tension and the point of no return. Tension decreases during the falling action. In the resolution, any conflicts presented in the exposition are solved, and the story concludes. An informative text that is structured sequentially will often go in order from one step to the next.

2. In the **problem-solution** structure, authors identify a potential problem and suggest a solution. This form of writing is usually divided into two parts (the problem and the solution) and can be found in informational texts. For example, cell phone, cable, and satellite providers use this structure in manuals to help customers troubleshoot or identify problems with services or products.

3. When authors want to discuss similarities and differences between separate concepts, they arrange thoughts in a **comparison-contrast** paragraph structure. Venn diagrams are an effective graphic organizer for comparison-contrast structures because they feature two overlapping circles that can be used to organize similarities and differences. A comparison-contrast essay organizes one paragraph based on similarities and another based on differences. A comparison-contrast essay can also be arranged with the similarities and differences of individual traits addressed within individual paragraphs. Words such as *however*, *but*, and *nevertheless* help signal a contrast in ideas.

4. **Descriptive** writing structure is designed to appeal to your senses. Much like an artist who constructs a painting, good descriptive writing builds an image in the reader's mind by appealing to the five senses: sight, hearing, taste, touch, and smell. However, overly descriptive writing can become distracting; whereas sparse descriptions can make settings and characters seem flat. Good authors must strike a balance between the two and provide enough detail to enable the reader to really see and experience what is happening in the plot without distracting the reader with excessive details.

5. Passages that use the **cause and effect** structure are simply asking *why* by demonstrating some type of connection between ideas. Words such as *if, since, because, then, or consequently* indicate a cause-and-effect relationship. By switching the order of a complex sentence, the writer can rearrange the emphasis on different clauses. Saying, *If Sheryl is late, we'll miss the dance*, is different from saying *We'll miss the dance if Sheryl is late*. One emphasizes Sheryl's tardiness while the other emphasizes missing the dance. Paragraphs can also be arranged in a cause and effect format. Cause-and-effect writing discusses the impact of decisions that have been made or could be made. Researchers often apply this paragraph structure to the scientific method.

Point of View

Point of view is an important writing device to consider. In fiction writing, point of view refers to who tells the story or from whose perspective readers are observing the story. In non-fiction writing, the **point of view** refers to whether the author refers to himself/herself, their readers, or chooses not to mention either. Whether fiction or nonfiction, the author will carefully consider the impact the perspective will have on the purpose and main point of the writing.

- **First-person point of view**: The story is told from the writer's perspective. In fiction, this would mean that the main character is also the narrator. First-person point of view is easily recognized by the use of personal pronouns such as *I, me, we, us, our, my*, and *myself*.

- **Third-person point of view**: In a more formal essay, this would be an appropriate perspective because the focus should be on the subject matter, not the writer or the reader.

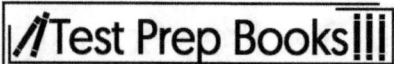

- **Third-person limited** point of view refers to a story told by a narrator who has access to the thoughts and feelings of just one character.

- In **third-person omniscient** point of view, the narrator has access to the thoughts and feelings of all the characters.

- In **third-person objective** point of view, the narrator is like a fly on the wall and can see and hear what the characters do and say but does not have access to their thoughts and feelings.

- **Second-person point of view:** This point of view isn't commonly used in fiction or nonfiction writing because it directly addresses the reader using the pronouns *you*, *your*, and *yourself*. Second-person perspective is more appropriate in direct communication, such as business letters or emails.

Third-person point of view is recognized by the use of the pronouns *he, she, they,* and *it*. In fiction writing, third-person point of view has a few variations.

Point of View	Pronouns Used
First person	I, me, we, us, our, my, myself
Second person	You, your, yourself
Third person	He, she, it, they

Main Ideas and Supporting Details

Topics and main ideas are critical parts of writing. The **topic** is the subject matter of the piece. An example of a topic would be *global warming*.

The main idea is what the writer wants to say about that topic. A writer may make the point that global warming is a growing problem that must be addressed in order to save the planet. Therefore, the topic is global warming, and the main idea is that it's *a serious problem needing to be addressed*. The topic can be expressed in a word or two, but the main idea should be a complete thought.

An author will likely identify the topic immediately within the title or the first sentence of a passage. The main idea is usually presented in the introduction. In a single passage, the main idea may be identified in the first or last sentence, but it will most likely be directly stated and easily recognized by the reader. Because it is not always stated immediately in a passage, it's important to carefully read the entire passage to identify the main idea.

The main idea should not be confused with the thesis statement. A **thesis statement** is a clear statement of the writer's specific stance and can often be found in the introduction of a non-fiction piece. The thesis is a specific sentence (or two) that offers the direction and focus of the discussion.

In order to illustrate the main idea, a writer will use **supporting details**, the details that provide evidence or examples to help make a point. Supporting details often appear in the form of quotations, paraphrasing, or analysis. Authors should connect details and analysis to the main point.

For example, in the example of global warming, where the author's main idea is to show the seriousness of this growing problem and the need for change, the use of supporting details in this piece would be critical in effectively making that point. Supporting details used here might include statistics on an increase in global temperatures and studies showing the impact of global warming on the planet. The author could also include projections for future climate change in order to illustrate potential lasting effects of global warming.

It's important to evaluate the author's supporting details to be sure that they are credible, provide evidence of the author's point, and directly support the main idea. Though shocking statistics grab readers' attention, their use could be ineffective information in the piece. Details like this are crucial to understanding the passage and evaluating how well the author presents their argument and evidence.

Also remember that when most authors write, they want to make a point or send a message. This point or message of a text is known as the theme. Authors may state themes explicitly, like in *Aesop's Fables*. More often, especially in modern literature, readers must infer the theme based on text details. Usually after carefully reading and analyzing an entire text, the reader can identify the theme. Typically, the longer the piece, the more themes you will encounter, though often one theme dominates the rest, as evidenced by the author's purposeful revisiting of it throughout the passage.

Evaluating a Passage

Determining conclusions requires being an active reader, as a reader must make a prediction and analyze facts to identify a conclusion. There are a few ways to determine a logical conclusion, but careful reading is the most important. It's helpful to read a passage a few times, noting details that seem important to the piece. A reader should also identify key words in a passage to determine the logical conclusion or determination that flows from the information presented.

Textual evidence within the details helps readers draw a conclusion about a passage. **Textual evidence** refers to information—facts and examples that support the main point. Textual evidence will likely come from outside sources and can be in the form of quoted or paraphrased material. In order to draw a conclusion from evidence, it's important to examine the credibility and validity of that evidence as well as how (and if) it relates to the main idea.

If an author presents a differing opinion or a **counterargument** in order to refute it, the reader should consider how and why the information is being presented. It is meant to strengthen the original argument and shouldn't be confused with the author's intended conclusion, but it should also be considered in the reader's final evaluation.

Sometimes, authors explicitly state the conclusion they want readers to understand. Alternatively, a conclusion may not be directly stated. In that case, readers must rely on the implications to form a logical conclusion:

> On the way to the bus stop, Michael realized his homework wasn't in his backpack. He ran back to the house to get it and made it back to the bus just in time.

In this example, though it's never explicitly stated, it can be inferred that Michael is a student on his way to school in the morning. When forming a conclusion from implied information, it's important to read the text carefully to find several pieces of evidence to support the conclusion.

Summarizing is an effective way to draw a conclusion from a passage. A summary is a shortened version of the original text, written by the reader in their own words. Focusing on the main points of the original text and including only the relevant details can help readers reach a conclusion. It's important to retain the original meaning of the passage.

Like summarizing, **paraphrasing** can also help a reader fully understand different parts of a text. Paraphrasing calls for the reader to take a small part of the passage and list or describe its main points. Paraphrasing is more than rewording the original passage, though. It should be written in the reader's own words, while still retaining the meaning of the original source. This will indicate an understanding of the original source, yet still help the reader expand on their interpretation.

Readers should pay attention to the **sequence**, or the order in which details are laid out in the text, as this can be important to understanding its meaning as a whole. Writers will often use transitional words to help the reader understand the order of events and to stay on track. Words like *next, then, after*, and *finally* show that the order of events is important to the author. In some cases, the author omits these transitional words, and the sequence is implied. Authors may even purposely present the information out of order to make an impact or have an effect on the reader. An example might be when a narrative writer uses **flashback** to reveal information.

Responding to a Passage and Making Inferences

There are a few ways for readers to engage actively with the text, such as making inferences and predictions. An **inference** refers to a point that is implied (as opposed to directly stated) by the evidence presented:

> Bradley packed up all of the items from his desk in a box and said goodbye to his coworkers for the last time.

From this sentence, though it is not directly stated, readers can infer that Bradley is leaving his job. It's necessary to use inference in order to draw conclusions about the meaning of a passage. Authors make implications through character dialogue, thoughts, effects on others, actions, and looks. Like in life, readers must assemble all the clues to form a complete picture.

When making an inference about a passage, it's important to rely only on the information that is provided in the text itself. This helps readers ensure that their conclusions are valid.

Readers will also find themselves making predictions when reading a passage or paragraph. **Predictions** are guesses about what's going to happen next. Readers can use prior knowledge to help make accurate predictions. Prior knowledge is best utilized when readers make links between the current text, previously read texts, and life experiences. Some texts use suspense and foreshadowing to captivate readers:

A cat darted across the street just as the car came careening around the curve.

One unfortunate prediction might be that the car will hit the cat. Of course, predictions aren't always accurate, so it's important to read carefully to the end of the text to determine the accuracy of predictions.

Verbal Reasoning

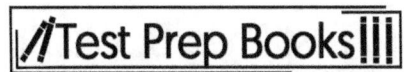

Critical Reasoning

It's important to read any piece of writing critically. In the Critical Reasoning sections of the GMAT Focus Edition, individuals will be tested on their ability to make arguments, evaluate arguments, and create or correct a plan of action.

To evaluate an argument, the goal is to discover the point and purpose of what the author is writing about through analysis. It's also crucial to establish the point or stance the author has taken on the topic of the piece. After determining the author's perspective, readers can then more effectively develop their own viewpoints on the subject of the piece.

In most of the Critical Reasoning section, test takers will face questions that ask them to read a short text, evaluate the argument, and then select which answer choice either strengthens or weakens the argument, tells why the argument is flawed, or strongly supports or damages the argument. Test takers will not need specialized knowledge of the content to answer these questions.

Here is an example of a critical reasoning question:

The United States' economy continues to grow. Over the last decade, the country's Gross Domestic Product—the monetary value of all finished goods and services produced within a country's borders—has increased by between 2 and 4 percent. The United States' economy is guaranteed to grow between 2 and 4 percent next year.

The flawed reasoning in which of the following arguments most mirrors the flawed reasoning presented in the argument above?

a. Ted is obsessed with apple pie. He's consumed one whole pie every day for the last decade. Ted will probably eat a whole apple pie tomorrow.
b. Last year Alexandra finished as the top salesperson at her company. She will undoubtedly be the top salesperson next year.
c. George always brushes his teeth right before getting into bed. His bedtime routine has remained the same for two decades. It's more probable than not that George brushes his teeth right before getting into bed tomorrow night.
d. Germany's economy is the strongest it's been since the end of World War II. Over the last decade, the country's Gross Domestic Product—the monetary value of all finished goods and services produced within a country's borders—has increased by between 2 and 4 percent. Germany's economic growth is a result of inclusive democratic processes.
e. Tito is the top ranked surfer in the world. Las Vegas bookmakers listed him as a clear favorite to win the upcoming invitational tournament. Tito is more likely to win the invitational than any other surfer.

The question presents a situation and ask test takers to select an answer choice that mirrors the flawed reasoning in the argument. When solving these types of questions, test takers should read through every answer choice to find the one that aligns best with the question.

In this case, Choice *B* is the correct answer choice. Like the argument, it takes past events and speculates that conditions will not change. Just as any number of factors could alter the United States' economic growth, it is similarly unreasonable to say that Alexandra will be the top salesperson based on one year's

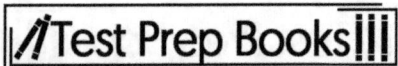

data. This answer choice also uses extremely strong language in its speculation (*guaranteed* and *undoubtedly*).

Choice *A* is similar to the argument in that it makes a prediction based on past events; however, Choice *A*'s argument is much more reasonable than the argument. If Ted has eaten an apple pie every day for the last decade, then it's reasonable to assume that he will do so again tomorrow.

Choice *C* is similar to the argument, but its conclusion is much more reasonable. If George has brushed his teeth right before bed for twenty years, then it is not unreasonable to speculate that he will do the same tonight. This is not the same as predicting that past economic conditions will continue into the future. George has much more control over brushing his teeth than the United States has over its economy.

Choice *D* mirrors the language as the argument, but it draws a very different conclusion. In contrast to the argument, Choice *D*'s conclusion gives a reason why Germany's economy is on the rise. It does not make a guarantee of future growth. This is not the same as the argument.

Choice *E* does not rely on flawed reasoning, so it must be incorrect. If Tito is the top ranked surfer in the world and listed as a clear favorite, then it's true that he's the most likely to win the tournament.

Therefore, Choice *B* is the correct answer, and it's confirmed by the fact that all of the other answer choices are incorrect.

Critical Thinking Skills

Critical readers examine the facts used to support an author's argument. They check the facts against other sources to be sure those facts are correct. They also check the validity of the sources used to be sure those sources are credible, academic, and/or peer reviewed. Consider that when an author uses another person's opinion to support their argument, even if it is an expert's opinion, it is still only an opinion and should not be taken as fact. A strong argument uses valid, measurable facts to support ideas. Even then, the reader may disagree with the argument as it may be rooted in their personal beliefs.

An authoritative argument may use the facts to sway the reader. Because of this, a writer may choose to only use the information and expert opinion that supports their viewpoint.

If the argument is that wind energy is the best solution, the author will use facts that support this idea. That same author may leave out relevant facts on solar energy. The way the author uses facts can influence the reader, so it's important to consider the facts being used, how those facts are being presented, and what information might be left out.

Critical readers should also look for errors in the argument such as logical fallacies and bias. A **logical fallacy** is a flaw in the logic used to make the argument. Logical fallacies include slippery slope, straw man, and begging the question. Authors can also reflect **bias** if they ignore an opposing viewpoint or present their side in an unbalanced way. A strong argument considers the opposition and finds a way to refute it. Critical readers should look for an unfair or one-sided presentation of the argument and be skeptical, as a bias may be present. Even if this bias is unintentional, if it exists in the writing, the reader should be wary of the validity of the argument.

Readers should also look for the use of **stereotypes**. These are the overly simplified beliefs about a person, place, thing, etc. that is indiscriminately applied to a larger group. These can be positive but are usually negative in nature. When a reader comes across the use of stereotypes, they should take that into consideration as they analyze the author's argument. These should generally be avoided. Stereotypes reveal a flaw in the writer's thinking and may suggest a lack of knowledge or understanding about the subject.

Constructing Arguments Through Evidence

Using only one form of supporting evidence is not nearly as effective as using a variety to support a claim. Presenting only a list of statistics can be boring to the reader, but providing a true story that's both interesting and humanizing helps. In addition, one example isn't always enough to prove the writer's larger point, so combining it with other examples in the writing is extremely effective. Thus, when reading a passage, readers should not just look for a single form of supporting evidence.

For example, although most people can't argue with the statement, "Seat belts save lives," its impact on the reader is much greater when supported by additional content. The writer can support this idea by:

- Providing statistics on the rate of highway fatalities alongside statistics of estimated seat belt usage.

- Explaining the science behind car accidents and what happens to a passenger who doesn't use a seat belt.

- Offering anecdotal evidence or true stories from reliable sources on how seat belts prevent fatal injuries in car crashes.

Another key aspect of supporting evidence is a **reliable source**. Does the writer include the source of the information? If so, is the source well-known and trustworthy? Is there a potential for bias? For example, a seat belt study done by a seat belt manufacturer may have its own agenda to promote.

Tone

Tone refers to the writer's attitude toward the subject matter. Tone is usually explained in terms of a work of fiction. For example, the tone conveys how the writer feels about their characters and the situations in which they're involved.

A lot of nonfiction writing has a neutral tone, which is an important tone for the writer to take. A neutral tone demonstrates that the writer is presenting a topic impartially and letting the information speak for itself. On the other hand, nonfiction writing can be just as effective and appropriate if the tone isn't neutral. For instance, take this example involving seat belts:

> Seat belts save more lives than any other automobile safety feature. Many studies show that airbags save lives as well; however, not all cars have airbags. For instance, some older cars don't. Furthermore, air bags aren't entirely reliable. For example, studies show that in 15% of accidents airbags don't deploy as designed, but, on the other hand, seat belt malfunctions are extremely rare. The number of highway fatalities has plummeted since laws requiring seat belt usage were enacted.

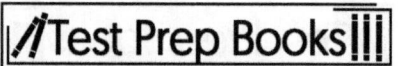

In this passage, the writer mostly chooses to retain a neutral tone when presenting information. If the writer would instead include their own personal experience of losing a friend or family member in a car accident, the tone would change dramatically. The tone would no longer be neutral and would show that the writer has a personal stake in the content, allowing them to interpret the information in a different way. When analyzing tone, consider what the writer is trying to achieve in the text and how they *create* the tone using style.

Data Insights

Data Sufficiency

Test takers should expect to see data sufficiency problems in the Data Insights section of the GMAT Focus Edition. For these questions, rather than needing to apply quantitative reasoning methods to explicitly solve the problem, test takers must review the provided information in relation to the posed question and determine if the provided information is sufficient to answer the question.

The data sufficiency questions provide a problem and then two statements labeled 1 and 2. Following this information, five answer choices, which will be identical for all data sufficiency questions, are presented.

Test takers must select the single valid choice for each data sufficiency question from the following five options:

A. Statement (1) ALONE is sufficient, but statement (2) alone is not sufficient to answer the question asked.
B. Statement (2) ALONE is sufficient, but statement (1) alone is not sufficient to answer the question asked.
C. BOTH statements (1) and (2) TOGETHER are sufficient to answer the question asked, but NEITHER statement ALONE is sufficient to answer the question asked.
D. EACH statement ALONE is sufficient to answer the question asked.
E. Statements (1) and (2) TOGETHER are NOT sufficient to answer the question asked, and additional data specific to the problem are needed.

Essentially, test takers must determine if just statement 1 *or* statement 2 alone provide enough information to solve the problem, if both statements are needed to arrive at the answer, if either has enough information (such that statement 1 could be used alone to solve the problem or statement 2 alone, but both aren't necessary), or if the problem cannot be solved even with all of the information put together from both.

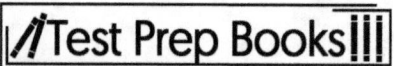

Data Insights

The flowchart that follows visually depicts the thinking process required by data sufficiency questions:

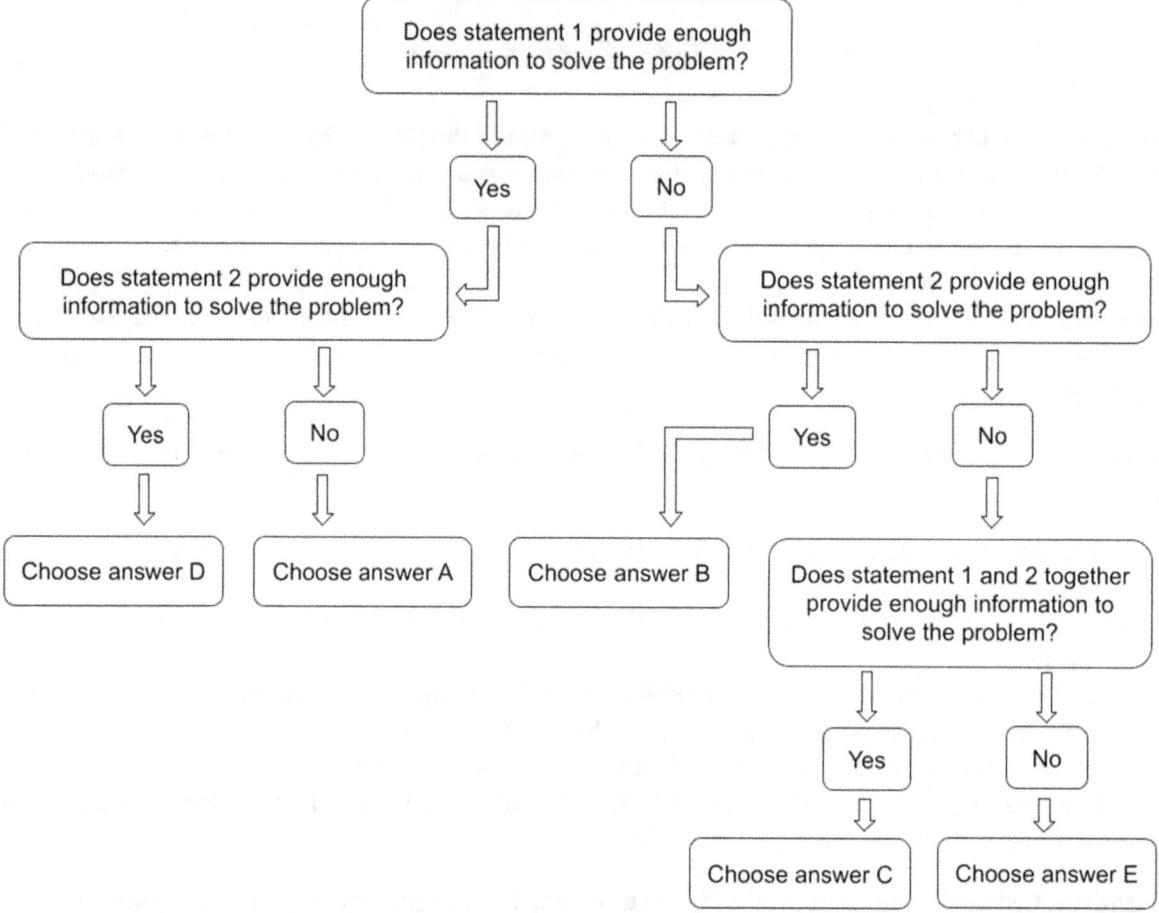

The good news is that test takers should not need to read through each of the five answer choices for every data sufficiency question because they will always be exactly the same and in the same order. By memorizing the answer options, test takers can save some time and bank it to use on actually working through the problems themselves. It is usually time efficient to consider statement 1 in isolation first, then statement 2, and determine if either alone provides information sufficient to solve the problem, or if both are needed. It is important for test takers to take the time to evaluate if either statement can be used in isolation to solve the problem and not just select one of the two because Choice *D* states that statement 1 alone *and* statement 2 alone contain enough information to solve the problem.

Graphics Interpretation

Identifying Information from a Graphic

Texts may have graphic representations to help illustrate and visually support assertions made. For example, graphics can be used to express samples or segments of a population or demonstrate growth or decay. Four of the most popular graphic formats include tables, bar graphs, line graphs, and pie charts.

Data Insights

Line graphs rely on a horizontal X-axis and a vertical Y-axis to establish baseline values. A point is plotted for each data value where the x-value and y-value of the data point intersect the axes, and those points are connected with lines. Compared to bar graphs or pie charts, line graphs are more useful for looking at the past and present and predicting future outcomes. For instance, a potential investor would look for stocks that demonstrated steady growth over many decades when examining the stock market. Note that severe spikes up and down indicate instability, while line graphs that display a slow but steady increase may indicate good returns.

Table Analysis

One of the most common ways to express data is in a table. The primary reason for plugging data into a table is to make interpretation more convenient. It's much easier to look at the table than to analyze results in a narrative paragraph. When analyzing a table, pay close attention to the title, variables, and data.

Let's analyze a theoretical antibiotic study. The study has 6 groups, named A through F, and each group receives a different dose of medicine. The results of the study are listed in the table below.

Results of Antibiotic Studies		
Group	Dosage of Antibiotics in milligrams (mg)	Efficacy (% of participants cured)
A	0 mg	20%
B	20 mg	40%
C	40 mg	75%
D	60 mg	95%
E	80 mg	100%
F	100 mg	100%

Tables generally list the title immediately above the data. The title should succinctly explain what is listed below. Here, "Results of Antibiotic Studies" informs the audience that the data pertains to the results of a scientific study on antibiotics.

Identifying the variables at play is one of the most important parts of interpreting data. Remember, the independent variable is intentionally altered, and its change is independent of the other variables. Here, the dosage of antibiotics administered to the different groups is the independent variable. The study is intentionally manipulating the strength of the medicine to study the related results. Efficacy is the dependent variable since its results *depend* on a different variable, the dose of antibiotics. Generally, the independent variable will be listed before the dependent variable in tables.

Also, pay close attention to the variables' labels. Here, the dose is expressed in milligrams (mg) and efficacy in percentages (%). Keep an eye out for questions referencing data in a different unit measurement or questions asking for a raw number when only the percentage is listed.

Now that the nature of the study and variables at play have been identified, the data itself needs be interpreted. Group A did not receive any of the medicine. As discussed earlier, Group A is the control, as it reflects the amount of people cured in the same timeframe without medicine. It's important to see that efficacy positively correlates with the dosage of medicine. A question using this study might ask for the lowest dose of antibiotics to achieve 100% efficacy. Although Group E and Group F both achieve 100% efficacy, it's important to note that Group E reaches 100% with a lower dose.

Bar Graphs

Here's an example of a bar graph:

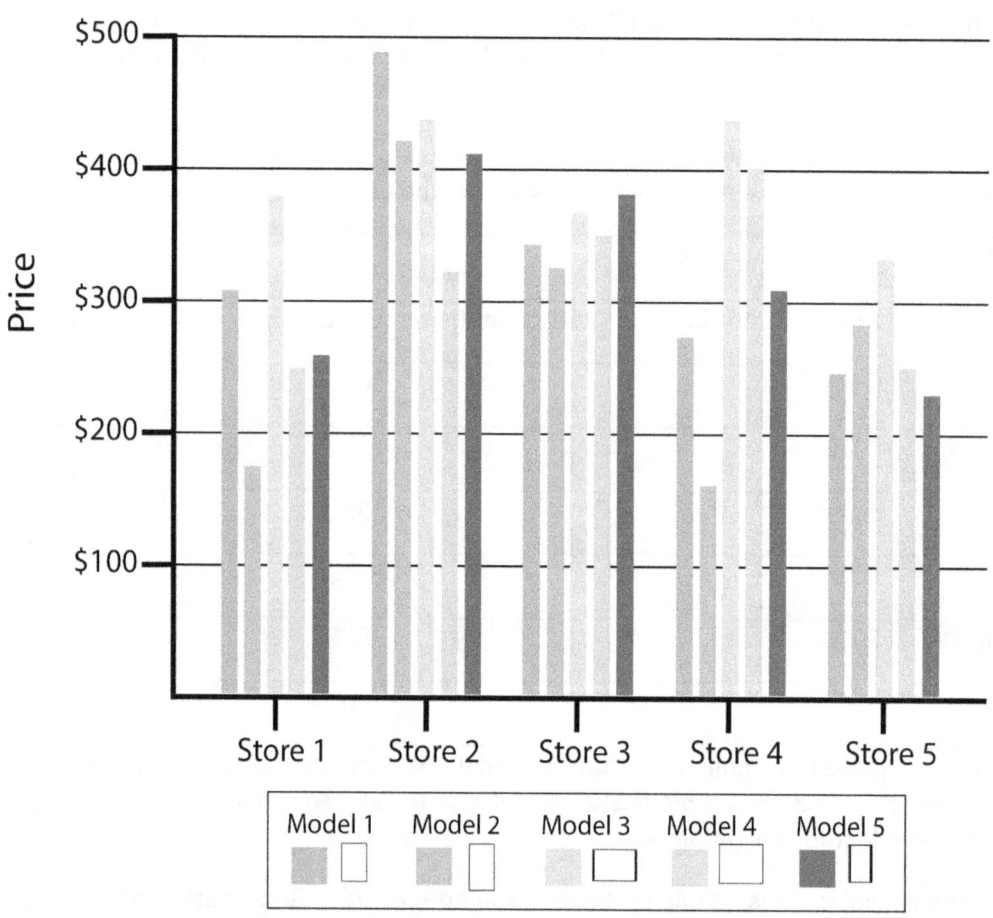

Bar graphs are usually displayed on a vertical Y-axis. The bars themselves can be two- or three-dimensional, depending on the designer's tastes. Unlike a line graph, which shows the fluctuation of only one variable, the X-axis on a bar graph is excellent for making comparisons because it shows differences between several variables. For instance, if an electronics store wanted to visually represent the number tablet sales for the year, a bar graph could have a bar for each type of tablet offered. To provide additional information, the store could show quarterly sales by constructing a bar for each type of tablet for each quarter in the fiscal year. The height of the bar would indicate the number of sales. The tablet types would be displayed along the x-axis with groups of four bars per tablet—one for each quarter.

Data Insights

Line Graphs

Like a scatter plot, a **line graph** compares variables that change continuously, typically over time. Paired data values (ordered pair) are plotted on a coordinate grid with the x- and y-axis representing the variables. A line is drawn from each point to the next, going from left to right. The line graph below displays cell phone use for given years (two variables) for men, women, and both sexes (three data sets).

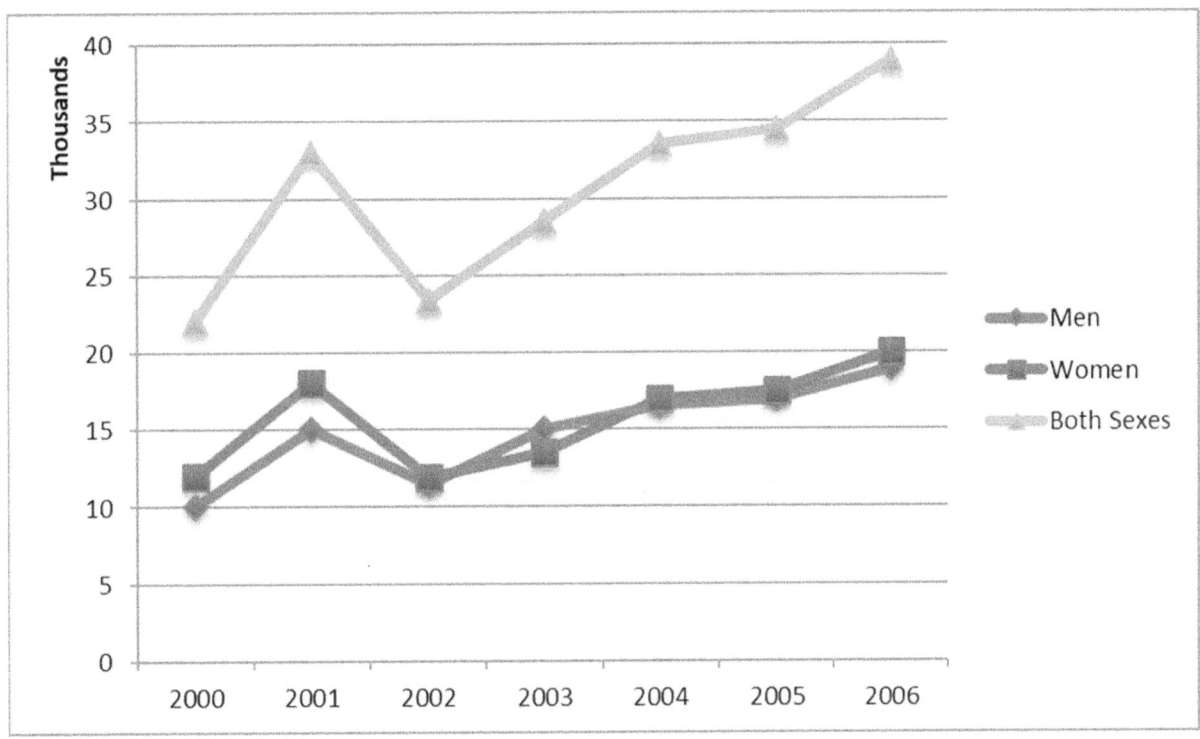

X/Y Graphs

When a linear equation is written in standard form, $Ax + By = C$, it is easy to identify the x- and y-intercepts for the graph of the line. Just as the y-intercept is the point at which the line intercepts the y-axis, the x-intercept is the point at which the line intercepts the x-axis. At the y-intercept, $x = 0$, and at the x-intercept, $y = 0$. Given an equation in standard form, substitute $x = 0$ to find the y-intercept, and substitute $y = 0$ to find the x-intercept. For example, to graph $3x + 2y = 6$, substituting 0 for y results in $3x + 2(0) = 6$. Solving for x yields $x = 2$; therefore, an ordered pair for the line is $(2, 0)$. Substituting

0 for x results in $3(0) + 2y = 6$. Solving for y yields $y = 3$; therefore, an ordered pair for the line is $(0, 3)$. Plot the two ordered pairs (the x- and y-intercepts), and construct a straight line through them.

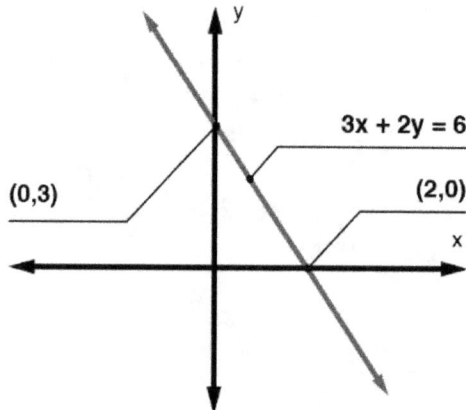

Data Insights

Recognizing Relationships in the Information

Pie Charts

A pie chart can depict multiple layers of information, especially when compared against other similarly constructed charts.

For example, the following pie charts can demonstrate sizable amounts of data over the course of time.

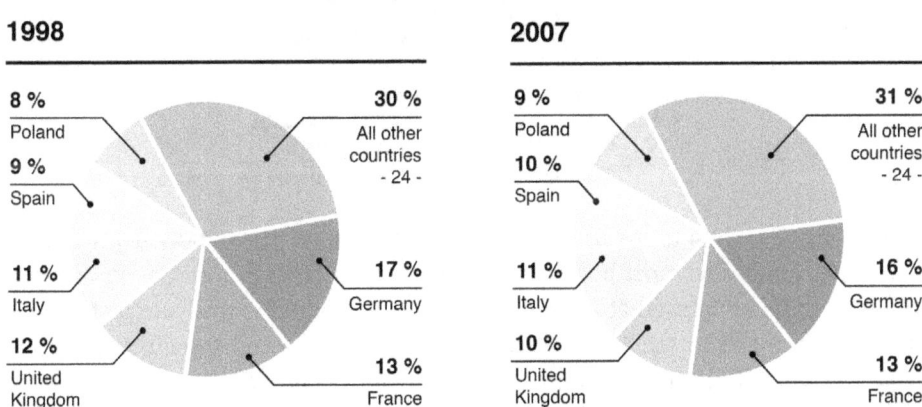

When putting such charts next to each other, it is easy to look at similarities and differences over the course of time, or among elements of the charts. The importance of such tools is observed in the ease of comparing multiple strings of data at once rather than being limited to simply one or two variables.

Relationships between similar measures can provide insight into correlations from year to year or product to product.

For example, the following graph can show a close positive correlation between the time students spend studying and their grades. This means that as the time spent studying increases, the students' grades also increase.

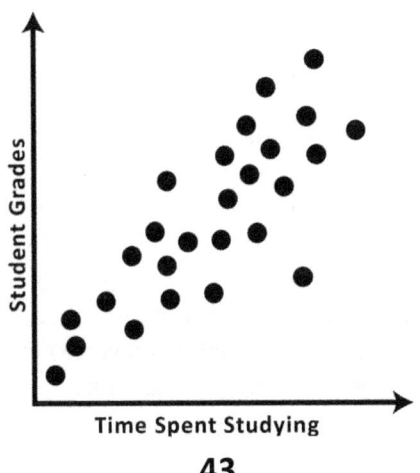

There can also be a negative correlation between variables. For example, the following graph shows a negative correlation between the number of missed classes and a student's exam score. It can be observed that the more classes a student misses, the lower the student's scores register.

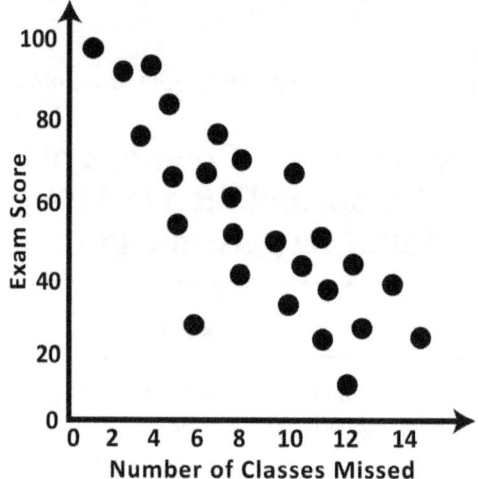

It can be a little less obvious when trying to identify relationships in information given via emails, or opinion-based writings. Generally, most business-based communications are dealing with a common topic that would need to be addressed at a meeting, such as a product, a marketing strategy, or production cost versus profit estimate. It can be difficult to decipher what the motivating factor might be for an employee's stance, but often the employee's role in the company can disclose what area he or she is going to regard as most important.

For example, a letter from the marketing expert in a company might discuss the best way to get a product out to the public and begin to register sales, while a financial expert for the same company may want to discuss the same product but discontinue its production due to the lack of profit potential compared to some unforeseen production costs. While both have the same topic in mind for discussion at a meeting, their stances on the future of the product differ. It is important to analyze any information given by each person's writing to understand their motivating factors and, thus, their position on a topic.

Multi-Source Reasoning

Multi-source reasoning questions on the GMAT Focus Edition measure test takers' abilities to use data from multiple sources and apply it real-world situations. The questions may involve recognizing data discrepancies, drawing inferences from the information, or determining relevant data.

When approaching the Data Sufficiency section of the GMAT Focus Edition, it is important to use all the information provided. Such information can be given from multiple sources, including tables, charts, graphs, and small excerpts from emails or articles. When viewing information, separate out key pieces, such as specific numbers that might determine a trend within a table or in a report of performance or sales. All sources should be labeled, thus making it easier to ascertain the relevance or importance of the data. Take an overall view of a table for the range of numbers and the headings of each column and row. On graphs or charts, the *x* and *y* axes (or horizontal and vertical lines) should be labeled with the value they are measuring, along with the base units for the measurements.

For example, the following position versus time graph is measured in meters per second, and the slope of the line can be determined to find the velocity.

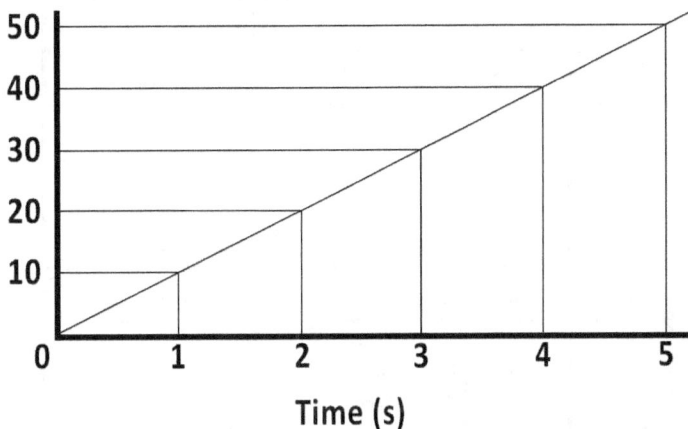

Time (s)

These pieces of information are used to determine past and future positions of the object being measured. A comparison of the movements of another object can determine trends in the positions of both objects.

The source of information from written dialogue, emails, or content can be used to determine the relevance of the material to the overall scope of the information. For example, an email from a company's marketing expert could contain more insight regarding a product's sales potential within a certain demographic compared to an email from a company's production manager. The source of the information determines the weight it should be given.

Manipulating Information from Multiple Sources to Solve Problems

Often data can be provided in a raw format that needs a bit of manipulation to find the desired answer. An example of this would be a table of data collected from an experiment or a survey taken from a sample. This type of data will often need to be rearranged so that comparisons can be made among the represented items. For example, the following information could be sorted in several ways to extrapolate specific information. The table could be sorted (as displayed) to determine the peak months for T-shirt purchases, or it could be re-sorted to determine the most purchased T-shirt size. Both pieces

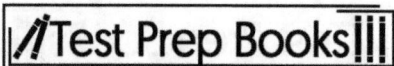

Data Insights

of information would come from the same data set, both would be important for production estimates, and both would require some manipulation of the information given.

	D	E	F
1	Payment	T-shirt Color	T-shirt Size
2	1 - Jan	Heather Gray	Large
3	1 - Jan	White	Large
4	4 - Jan	Dark Red	X - Large
5	5 - Jan	Dark Red	Medium
6	5 - Jan	Heather Gray	Large
7	5 - Jan	Dark Red	Medium
8	5 - Jan	Heather Gray	X - Large
9	6 - Jan	White	X - Large
10	6 - Jan	Dark Red	X - Large
11	7 - Jan	Heather Gray	Small
12	7 - Jan	Dark Red	Small
13	7 - Jan	Heather Gray	Small
14	7 - Jan	Heather Gray	Small
15	11 - Jan	Dark Red	Medium
16	11 - Jan	White	Medium
17	11 - Jan	Dark Red	Medium

In some cases, multiple pieces of information from various sources need to be used to assess a situation, solve a problem, or determine a sound course of action. For example, the following set of sources could be used to determine the best way for a small business to cater to its focus audience for advertising, sharing information, or simply networking. Each piece of information would need to be cross-referenced

Data Insights

from one set of tables to the other to match up the best social media source for the desired small business goal.

Social Media for Small Business Owners

Percentage of small businesses using the following in 2013

- 55 % Facebook
- 50 % Twitter
- 46 % LinkedIn
- 37 % None
- 30 % Pinterest
- 28 % Youtube
- 27 % Google+
- 16 % Instagram
- 10 % Blogs
- 6 % Foursquare

Percentage of small businesses using social media for:

- 75 % Business networking
- 52 % Keeping in touch with friends
- 21 % Political advocacy
- 6 % Other

Gathering information from multiple sources and then reapplying or manipulating it to make comparisons or estimates is the essence of what propels businesses. The importance of this can be seen in the cohesive branches of a business needing to communicate key pieces of information so the other branches can make decisions to further the company's overall goal. For instance, a T-shirt company needs to cross-reference production costs, availability of production products (such as textiles and dyes), implementation costs, employee costs and benefits, marketing strategies, and potential sales during both low and peak times. Additional promotions used for increasing sales could be observed and mapped onto existing data tables and manipulated to determine if the expense of the trial promotion produced enough profit to repeat.

Oftentimes, using information from multiple sources can assist with solving a basic problem. To hypothesize if a new idea would be profitable, it is recommended that some research be done to see if there are any types of similar productions, promotions, marketing, etc. This would require conducting a type of literature review and extracting any pertinent information that could be applied and manipulated to make estimates or predictions toward the idea being developed.

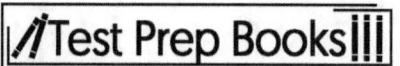

Data Insights

This requires a great deal of comparisons across multiple venues. When looking to make such comparisons, existing data is not always in the exact form necessary to draw a solid conclusion. Therefore, the research much be augmented by any predicted standard deviations or alternative results that could arise. This should include being able to make some predictions for plans a business might have involving the idea. For example, if a toy company wanted to produce a new toy that involved wheels, they would need to research similar toys that use the same type/size of wheels and decide if there were age restrictions for users, cost restrictions for production, durability restrictions for the use of the toy, and the overall aesthetics involved with the existing toys that use that type of wheel. This kind of information manipulation could aid in cutting costs, focusing marketing, and avoiding safety issues.

Two-Part Analysis

A few of the questions in the Data Analysis section will be two-part analysis questions. This requires test takers to solve complex problems that will have two answers. The questions may offer a short paragraph, a mathematical problem, or a mixture of both that test takers will evaluate and solve.

Here is an example of a two-part analysis question:

The quotient $\frac{x}{y}$ is a multiple of 7.

In the table below, choose the value of x and the value of y that are consistent with this statement. Make only one selection for x and one selection for y.

x	y	
○	○	72
○	○	119
○	○	1,296
○	○	13

The correct value for x is 1,176 and the correct value for y is 56 because $\frac{1176}{56} = 21$, which is a multiple of 7 because:

$$3 \times 7 = 21$$

Many two-part analysis questions will require test takers to try multiple answers to find out which one is right. Any of the other number combinations would have resulted in an answer that is not a multiple of 7, making them incorrect.

Take time to make sure that the correct answer is selected for the correct section, for example: the bubble under x should be filled at 1,176, and the bubble under y should be filled at 56. The opposite way would result in an answer of $\frac{1}{7}$, which is incorrect.

Practice Test #1

Quantitative Reasoning

Problem Solving

1. Which of the following numbers has the greatest value?
    a. 1.43785
    b. 1.07548
    c. 1.43592
    d. 0.89409
    e. 1.42688

2. The value of 6 × 12 is the same as:
    a. 2 × 4 × 4 × 2
    b. 7 × 4 × 3
    c. 6 × 6 × 3
    d. 3 × 2 × 4 × 3
    e. 3 × 4 × 6 × 2

3. Because of an increase in demand, the price of a designer purse has increased 25% from the original price of $128. What is the new price of the purse?
    a. $32
    b. $102
    c. $192
    d. $96
    e. $160

4. After a 20% sale discount, Frank purchased a new refrigerator for $850. How much money did he save off of the original price?
    a. $170
    b. $212.50
    c. $105.75
    d. $200
    e. $150

5. A student gets an 85% on a test with 20 questions. How many questions did the student solve correctly?
    a. 16
    b. 15
    c. 18
    d. 19
    e. 17

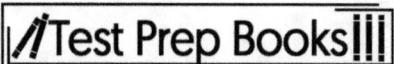

6. Alan currently weighs 200 pounds, but he wants to lose weight to get down to 175 pounds. What is this difference in kilograms? (1 pound is approximately equal to 0.45 kilograms.)
   a. 9 kg
   b. 11.25 kg
   c. 78.75 kg
   d. 90 kg
   e. 25 kg

7. Johnny earns $2,334.50 from his job each month. He pays $1,437 for monthly expenses and saves the rest. Johnny is planning a vacation in 3 months that he estimates will cost $1,750 total. How much will Johnny have left over from 3 months of saving once he pays for his vacation?
   a. $948.50
   b. $584.50
   c. $852.50
   d. $942.50
   e. $952.50

8. What is $\frac{420}{98}$ rounded to the nearest integer?
   a. 3
   b. 4
   c. 5
   d. 6
   e. 7

9. Dwayne has received the following scores on his math tests: 78, 92, 83, 97. What score must Dwayne get on his next math test to have an overall average of 90?
   a. 89
   b. 98
   c. 95
   d. 100
   e. 96

10. What is the overall median of Dwayne's current scores: 78, 92, 83, 97?
    a. 19
    b. 85
    c. 83
    d. 87.5
    e. 86

11. Solve the following:

$$(\sqrt{36} \times \sqrt{16}) - 3^2$$

   a. 30
   b. 21
   c. 15
   d. 13
   e. 16

12. In Jim's school, there are a total of 650 students. There are three girls for every two boys. How many students are girls?
   a. 260
   b. 130
   c. 65
   d. 390
   e. 225

13. Five of six numbers have a sum of 25. The average of all six numbers is 6. What is the sixth number?
   a. 8
   b. 12
   c. 13
   d. 10
   e. 11

14. Kimberley earns $10 an hour babysitting, and after 10 p.m., she earns $12 an hour. The time she works is rounded to the nearest hour for pay purposes. On her last job, she worked from 5:30 p.m. to 11:00 p.m. In total, how much did Kimberley earn on her last job?
   a. $45
   b. $57
   c. $62
   d. $42
   e. $67

15. A store is having a sale on jackets and boots. The jackets are on sale for $47 each, and the boots are on sale for $38 for each pair. How much would it cost to buy 2 jackets and 3 pairs of boots?
   a. $208
   b. $114
   c. $94
   d. $217
   e. $170

16. Arrange the following numbers from least to greatest value:

$$0.85, \frac{4}{5}, \frac{2}{3}, \frac{91}{100}$$

   a. $0.85, \frac{4}{5}, \frac{2}{3}, \frac{91}{100}$
   b. $\frac{4}{5}, 0.85, \frac{91}{100}, \frac{2}{3}$
   c. $\frac{2}{3}, \frac{4}{5}, 0.85, \frac{91}{100}$
   d. $0.85, \frac{91}{100}, \frac{4}{5}, \frac{2}{3}$
   e. $\frac{4}{5}, \frac{2}{3}, 0.85, \frac{91}{100}$

17. Keith's bakery had 252 customers go through its doors last week. This week, that number increased to 378. Express this increase as a percentage.
    a. 26%
    b. 50%
    c. 35%
    d. 12%
    e. 28%

18. If 40% of y is 24, then y is what percent of 120?
    a. 30%
    b. 40%
    c. 50%
    d. 60%
    e. 70%

19. Four people split a bill. The first person pays for $\frac{1}{5}$, the second person pays for $\frac{1}{4}$, and the third person pays for $\frac{1}{3}$. What fraction of the bill does the fourth person pay?
    a. $\frac{13}{60}$
    b. $\frac{47}{60}$
    c. $\frac{1}{4}$
    d. $\frac{4}{15}$
    e. $\frac{1}{2}$

20. Simplify the following expression:
$$4\frac{2}{3} - 3\frac{4}{9}$$
    a. $1\frac{1}{3}$
    b. $1\frac{2}{9}$
    c. 1
    d. $1\frac{2}{3}$
    e. $1\frac{4}{9}$

21. A closet is filled with red, blue, and green shirts. If $\frac{1}{3}$ of the shirts are green and $\frac{2}{5}$ are red, what fraction of the shirts are blue?

   a. $\frac{4}{15}$
   b. $\frac{1}{5}$
   c. $\frac{7}{15}$
   d. $\frac{1}{2}$
   e. $\frac{2}{3}$

Verbal Reasoning

Reading Comprehension

Questions 1–4 are based on the following passage:

The town of Alexandria, Virginia was founded in 1749. Between the years 1810 and 1861, this thriving seaport was the ideal location for slave owners such as Joseph Bruin, Henry Hill, Isaac Franklin, and John Armfield to build several slave trade office structures, including slave holding areas. After 1830, when the manufacturing-based economy slowed down in Virginia, slaves were traded to plantations in the Deep South, in Alabama, Mississippi, and Louisiana. Joseph Bruin, one of the most notorious of the slave traders operating in Alexandria, alone purchased hundreds of slaves from 1844 to 1861. Harriet Beecher Stowe claimed that the horrible slave traders mentioned in her novel, *Uncle Tom's Cabin*, are reminiscent of the coldhearted Joseph Bruin. The Franklin and Armfield Office was known as one of the largest slave trading companies in the country up to the end of the Civil War period. Slaves, waiting to be traded, were held in a two-story slave pen built behind the Franklin and Armfield Office structure on Duke Street in Alexandria. Yet, many people fought to thwart these traders and did everything they could to rescue and free slaves. Two Christian African American slave sisters, with the help of northern abolitionists who bought their freedom, escaped Bruin's plan to sell them into southern prostitution. In 1861, Joseph Bruin was captured and imprisoned and his property confiscated. The Bruin Slave Jail became the Fairfax County courthouse until 1865. The original Franklin and Armfield Office building still stands in Virginia and is registered in the National Register of Historic Places. The Bruin Slave Jail is still standing on Duke Street in Alexandria but is not open to the public. The history of the slave trading enterprise is preserved and presented to the public by the Northern Virginia Urban League.

1. Based on the above passage, which of the following statements about the town of Alexandria are true?
    a. Alexandria was a seaport town that could not prosper, even with the advent of a slave trade business, because the manufacturing industry was not enough to stabilize the economy.
    b. Slave traders such as Joseph Bruin, Henry Hill, Isaac Franklin, and John Armfield rented both slave trade office buildings and slave holding buildings from landlords of Old Town, Alexandria.
    c. For over fifteen years, Joseph Bruin, a notorious slave trader, probably the one characterized in *Uncle Tom's Cabin*, bought hundreds of slaves with the intention of sending the purchased slaves to southern states such as Alabama, Mississippi, and Louisiana.
    d. The Bruin Slave Jail is open to the public; the building is located in downtown Alexandria, and still stands in Virginia. The jail is registered in the National Register of Historic Places. The history of the slave trading enterprise is preserved and presented to the public by the Northern Virginia Urban League.
    e. Isaac Franklin and John Armfield's slave-trade office structures, including slave holding areas in downtown Alexandria, did not remain open for their slave trade business until the end of the Civil War.

2. The passage about the Alexandria slave trade business suggests that which of the following statements can be regarded as true?
    a. The lucrative seaport town of Alexandria was supported by the successful slave trade businesses of men like Joseph Bruin, Henry Hill, Isaac Franklin, and John Armfield, who bought slaves and sold them to the plantations in the Deep South.
    b. Joseph Bruin, a highly respected Alexandrian businessman, ran a slave trade business in downtown Alexandria until the business closed its doors at the end of the Civil War.
    c. The Franklin and Armfield Office was built by Isaac Franklin and John Armfield. Slaves, waiting to be traded, were held in a four-story slave pen built behind the Franklin and Armfield Office structure on Duke Street in Alexandria.
    d. When the Confederate Army positioned its command in Alexandria and closed slave traders' businesses, the Franklin and Armfield slave pen became the Fairfax County courthouse and was used to hold Union soldiers.
    e. Literature about the slave trading enterprise, like *Uncle Tom's Cabin*, is being preserved and presented to the public by the Northern Virginia Urban League.

3. Which of the following statements are accurate, based on the information provided in the passage?
    a. The town of Alexandria, founded in 1810, became one of the most infamous slave trading markets in the country.
    b. Harriet Beecher Stowe was an escaped slave who was held in the Franklin and Armfield slave pen, located on Duke Street in Alexandria. To avoid a life as a prostitute, Miss Stowe tried to escape from the control of Joseph Bruin, whose surly characteristics surfaced in her classic book, *Uncle Tom's Cabin*.
    c. Northern abolitionists were not known to help runaway slaves escape the hands of their notorious owners.
    d. The Bruin Slave Jail, located in downtown Alexandria, still stands today, although it is not open for public viewing.
    e. For convenience, the slave traders took their slaves to nearby Annapolis, Maryland, because the cost of shipping them from there was less than the cost of shipping them from Alexandria.

4. Which of the following statements best illustrates the author's intended main point or thesis?
   a. Two Christian African American slave sisters, with the help of northern abolitionists who bought their freedom, escaped Bruin's plan to sell them into southern prostitution.
   b. The town of Alexandria, a thriving seaport founded in 1749, was the location for several lucrative slave trading companies from 1810 to 1861.
   c. After the start of the Civil War, Joseph Bruin was captured and his jail was no longer used for his slave trade business.
   d. The Bruin Slave Jail is still standing on Duke Street in Alexandria but is not open to the public.
   e. In 1861, the Bruin Slave Jail in Alexandria became the Fairfax County courthouse.

Questions 5–9 are based on the following passage:

Becoming a successful leader in today's industry, government, and nonprofit sectors requires more than a high intelligence quotient (IQ). Emotional Intelligence (EI) includes developing the ability to know one's own emotions, to regulate impulses and emotions, and to use interpersonal communication skills with ease while dealing with other people. A combination of knowledge, skills, abilities, and mature EI reflects the most effective leadership recipe. Successful leaders sharpen more than their talents and IQ levels; they practice the basic features of EI. Some of the hallmark traits of a competent, emotionally intelligent leader include self-efficacy, drive, determination, collaboration, vision, humility, and openness to change. An unsuccessful leader exhibits opposite leadership traits: unclear directives, inconsistent vision and planning strategies, disrespect for followers, incompetence, and an uncompromising transactional leadership style. There are ways to develop emotional intelligence for the person who wants to improve their leadership style. For example, an emotionally intelligent leader creates an affirmative environment by incorporating collaborative activities, using professional development training for employee self-awareness, communicating clearly about the organization's vision, and developing a variety of resources for working with emotions. Building relationships outside the institution with leadership coaches and with professional development trainers can also help leaders who want to grow their leadership success. Leaders in today's work environment need to strive for a combination of skill, knowledge, and mature EI to lead followers to success and to promote the vision and mission of their respective institutions.

5. The passage suggests that the term *emotional intelligence (EI)* can be defined as which of the following?
   a. A combination of knowledge, skills, abilities, and mature EI reflects the most effective leader recipe.
   b. An emotionally intelligent leader creates an affirmative environment by incorporating collaborative activities, using professional development training for employee self-awareness, communicating clearly about the organization's vision, and developing a variety of resources for working with emotions.
   c. EI includes developing the ability to know one's own emotions, to regulate impulses and emotions, and to use interpersonal communication skills with ease while dealing with other people.
   d. Becoming a successful leader in today's industry, government, and nonprofit sectors requires more than a high intelligence quotient (IQ).
   e. Unclear directives, inconsistent vision and planning strategies, disrespect for followers, incompetence, and an uncompromising transactional leader style.

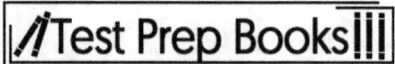

6. Based on the information in the passage, evaluate this statement: "A successful leader must have high EI."
    a. The above statement can be supported by the fact that Daniel Goldman conducted a scientific study.
    b. The above statement cannot be supported by the example that emotionally intelligent people are highly successful leaders.
    c. The above statement is supported by the passage.
    d. The above statement is not addressed in the passage
    e. The above statement can be inferred because emotionally intelligent people always make successful leaders.

7. According to the passage above, some of the characteristics of an unsuccessful leader include which of the following?
    a. Talent, IQ level, and abilities
    b. Humility, knowledge, and skills
    c. Loud, demeaning actions toward female employees
    d. Outdated technological resources and strategies
    e. Transactional leadership style

8. According to the passage above, which of the following must be true?
    a. A good leader exhibits a healthy work/life balance lifestyle.
    b. A good leader is uncompromising in transactional directives for all employees, regardless of status.
    c. A good leader learns to strategize using future trends analysis to create a five-year plan.
    d. A good leader uses a combination of skill, knowledge, and mature reasoning to make decisions.
    e. A good leader continually tries to improve their EI test quotient by studying the intelligence quotient of other successful leaders.

9. According to the passage above, which of the following choices are true?
    a. To be successful, leaders in the nonprofit sector need to develop neurological intelligence.
    b. It is not necessary for military leaders to develop emotional intelligence because they prefer a transactional leadership style.
    c. Leadership coaches cannot add value to someone who is developing their emotional intelligence.
    d. Humility is a valued character value; however, it is not necessarily a trademark of an emotionally intelligent leader.
    e. If a leader does not have the level of emotional intelligence required for a certain job, they are capable of increasing emotional intelligence.

Questions 10–14 are based on the following passage:

Learning how to write a 10-minute play may seem like a monumental task at first; but, if you follow a simple creative writing strategy, similar to the ones used for writing narrative stories, you will be able to write a successful drama. The first step is to open your story as if it is a puzzle to be solved. This will allow the reader a moment to engage with the story and to mentally solve the story with you, the author. You should immediately provide descriptive details that steer the main idea, the tone, and the mood according to the overarching theme you have in mind. For example, if the play is about something ominous, you may open scene one with a thunderclap. Next, use dialogue to reveal the attitudes and personalities of each of the characters who have a key part in the unfolding story. Keep the characters off balance in some way to create interest and dramatic effect. Maybe what the characters say does not match what they do. Show images on stage to speed up the narrative; remember, one picture speaks a thousand words. As the play progresses, the protagonist must cross the point of no return in some way; this is the climax of the story. Then, as in a written story, you create a resolution to the life-changing event of the protagonist. Let the characters experience some kind of self-discovery that can be understood and appreciated by the patient audience. Finally, make sure all things come together in the end so that every detail in the play makes sense right before the curtain falls.

10. Based on the passage above, which of the following statements is FALSE?
    a. Writing a 10-minute play may seem like an insurmountable task.
    b. Providing descriptive details is not necessary until after the climax of the storyline.
    c. Engaging the audience by jumping into the storyline immediately helps them solve the story's developing ideas with you, the writer.
    d. Descriptive details give clues to the play's intended mood and tone.
    e. The introduction of a ten-minute play does not need to open with a lot of coffee pouring or cigarette smoking to introduce the scenes. The action can get started right away.

11. Based on the passage above, which of the following is true?
    a. The class of eighth graders quickly learned that it is not that difficult to write a 10-minute play.
    b. The playwrights of the 21st century all use the narrative writing basic feature guide to outline their initial scripts.
    c. In order to follow a simple structure, a person can write a 10-minute play based on some narrative writing features.
    d. Women find playwriting easier than men because they are used to communicating in writing.
    e. The structure of writing a poem is similar to that of play writing and of narrative writing.

12. Based on your understanding of the passage above, it can be assumed that which of the following statements are true?
    a. One way to reveal the identities and nuances of the characters in a play is to use props.
    b. Characters should follow predictable routes in the challenge presented in the unfolding narrative, so the audience may easily follow the sequence of events.
    c. Using images in the stage design is an important element of creating atmosphere and meaning for the drama.
    d. There is no need for the protagonist to come to terms with a self-discovery; he or she simply needs to follow the prescription for life lived as usual.
    e. It is perfectly fine to avoid serious consequences for the actors of a ten-minute play because there is not enough time to unravel perils.

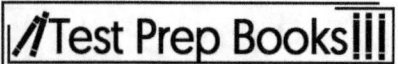

13. In the passage above, the writer suggests that writing a 10-minute play is accessible for a novice playwright because of which of the following reasons?
    a. It took the author of the passage only one week to write his first play.
    b. The format follows similar strategies of writing a narrative story.
    c. There are no particular themes or points to unravel; a playwright can use a stream of consciousness style to write a play.
    d. Dialogue that reveals the characters' particularities is uncommonly simple to write.
    e. The characters of a ten-minute play wrap up the action simply by revealing their ideas in a monologue.

14. Based on the passage above, which basic feature of narrative writing is NOT mentioned with respect to writing a 10-minute play?
    a. Character development
    b. Descriptive details
    c. Dialogue
    d. Mood and tone
    e. Style

Critical Reasoning

15. Dalton: Agribusiness is an industry that's polluting the world and causing greenhouse emissions as quickly as the oil and automobile industries combined. In order to reduce global warming, we should think about eating less of the types of foods that agribusiness sells.
Alexis: If we want to reduce global warming, we should seriously think about what kind of cars we drive.

Alexis' response to Dalton serves to do which of the following?
    a. Serves to reinforce Dalton's claims of the causes of global warming.
    b. Strengthens Dalton's argument by adding to it.
    c. Questions whether Dalton knows what he's talking about.
    d. Backs up Dalton's claims with more evidence of the causes of global warming.
    e. Suggest an alternative factor to the problem of global warming.

16. Shelby has fifteen years of coding experience. I thought that she would be the perfect fit for your company since you are looking for a proficient coder.
The speaker assumes which of the following?
    a. That Shelby is an excellent coder.
    b. That the company is looking for someone with fifteen years of experience.
    c. That Shelby will be a bad fit for the company.
    d. That fifteen years of experience makes someone a proficient coder.
    e. That Shelby is the best candidate for the job.

17. The "complete protein" is a source of protein that contains all nine of the essential amino acids necessary for our dietary needs. The complete protein is found in meat. Therefore, everyone should eat meat to fulfill their protein needs.
Which of the following, if true, would most weaken the above argument?
   a. Grass-fed beef is the most ethical way to buy meat to fulfill your protein needs.
   b. Legumes such as beans, seeds, or lentils mixed with grains such as pasta, rice, or corn creates a complete protein.
   c. Amino acids are necessary for humans to ingest; the body cannot make its own amino acids.
   d. Fruits and vegetables contain essential fiber, vitamins, and minerals that help our bodies fight disease.
   e. Everyone should eat more fats because they are good for your skin and hair, and help energize your body.

18. John looks like a professional bodybuilder. He weighs 210 pounds and stands six feet tall, which is the size of an NFL linebacker. John looks huge when he enters the room. Years of gym time have clearly paid off in spades.
Which of the following, if true, weakens the argument?
   a. John prefers to work out in the morning.
   b. The average professional bodybuilder is considerably heavier and taller than the average NFL linebacker.
   c. John weighed considerably less before he started working out.
   d. John's father, brothers, and male cousins all look like professional bodybuilders, and none of them have ever worked out.
   e. John works out five times every week.

19. Hank is a professional writer. He submits regular columns at two blogs and self-publishes romance novels. Hank recently signed with an agent based in New York. To date, Hank has never made any money off his writing.
The strength of the argument depends on which of the following?
   a. Hank's agent works at the biggest firm in New York.
   b. Being a professional writer requires representation by an agent.
   c. Hank's self-published novels and blogs have received generally positive reviews.
   d. Being a professional writer does not require earning money.
   e. Hank writes ten thousand words per day.

20. Quillium is the most popular blood pressure regulating prescription drug on the market. Giant Pharma, Inc., the largest prescription drug manufacturer in the country, owns the patent on Quillium. Giant Pharma stock is hitting unprecedented high valuations. As a result, Quillium is by far the most effective drug available in treating irregular blood pressure.
Which of the following, if true, most weakens the argument?
   a. The most lucrative and popular pharmaceuticals are not always the most effective.
   b. Quillium passed the FDA drug testing and screening faster than any other drug.
   c. Giant Pharma gouges its customers on Quillium's price.
   d. Giant Pharma's high stock prices are attributable to recent patent acquisitions other than Quillium.
   e. Quillium has numerous alternate applications.

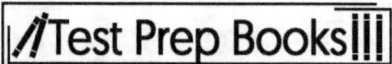

Practice Test #1

21. Julia joined Michael Scott Paperless Company, a small New York based tech start-up company, last month. Michael Scott Paperless recently received a valuation of ten million dollars. Julia is clearly the reason for the valuation.
Which of the following statements, if true, most weakens the argument?
   a. Michael Scott Paperless Company released an extremely popular mobile application shortly before hiring Julia.
   b. Michael Scott Paperless Company is wildly overvalued.
   c. Julia is an expert in her field.
   d. Julia only started working two weeks before the valuation.
   e. Julia completed two important projects during her first month with the company.

22. Advertisement: Cigarettes are deadly. Hundreds of thousands of people die every year from smoking-related causes, such as lung cancer or heart disease. The science is clear—smoking a pack per day for years will shorten one's life. Sitting in a room where someone is smoking might as well be a gas chamber in terms of damage to long-term health.
Which one of the following best describes the flaw in the author's reasoning?
   a. The advertisement confuses cause and effect.
   b. The advertisement uses overly broad generalization.
   c. The advertisement draws an unjustified analogy.
   d. The advertisement relies on shoddy science.
   e. The advertisement makes an unreasonable logical leap.

23. Jake works for Bank Conglomerate of America (BCA), the largest investment bank in the United States. Jake has worked at Bank Conglomerate of America for a decade. Every American investment bank employs dozens of lawyers to defend against insider-trading allegations. Some Bank Conglomerate of America employees must pass a certification course. However, all employees must complete a mandatory class on insider trading.
If the statements above are correct, which of the following must not be true?
   a. Jake took a class on insider trading.
   b. Jake passed a certification course.
   c. Jake has worked at Bank Conglomerate of America for a decade.
   d. Jake never took a class on insider trading.
   e. No investment bank has ever been formally charged with insider trading.

Data Insights

Multi-Source Reasoning

Prompt 1
Le Crème Ice Cream Company is popular in many Midwest states. The head of each department will be attending a meeting within the week. The following emails were circulated among the departments.

Email 1: Head of Marketing Department
The higher production costs of Blueberry Pie ice cream flavor have never been questioned due to it being one of the three most popular flavors Le Crème makes. With an increase in production costs, an adjustment in the marketing strategy could increase sales and profit. An idea for pairing the flavor with a

charitable donation per purchase could increase the interest, provide a reason to relaunch the flavor in the media and perhaps expand its targeted consumer base.

Email 2: Head of Production Department

Le Crème's Blueberry Pie ice cream flavor has always been the most expensive to produce. This has been in part due to the cost of the blueberries and also from using the private company Crusts for the specially sized pieces of pie crust blended into the flavor that do not break apart. With the over flooding on the growing season in Michigan, the blueberries are expected to be scarce, and the contract with Crusts is up for renewal. Both factors make it likely that the cost of production will increase. It might be time to renegotiate with both suppliers or seek out new suppliers. In the interim, we may need to make it a "seasonal" flavor, halt production, or discontinue the flavor altogether if we cannot secure new contracts.

Email 3: Company Owner

My family carefully developed the Blueberry Pie ice cream flavor in the tradition that Le Crème had always followed. The flavor has been a great seller from its inception. Its sales do not vary based upon seasonal demand like some of the less popular flavors such as Eggnog or Pumpkin. The contracted companies were selected for the refined flavors and specific constitution of their products. Altering any part of the recipe will indeed change the entire flavor. This company was founded on tradition and quality. We are not willing to sacrifice either for a minor bump in the road.

1. It can be inferred that:

   Yes   No

   O   O   All three individuals are focused on the continuance of the Blueberry Pie flavor.

   O   O   The Blueberry Pie flavor was one of the company's original flavors.

   O   O   The Blueberry Pie flavor is one of the company's top two selling flavors.

2. It can be inferred that:

   Yes   No

   O   O   One of the primary points of discussion at the next meeting will be the future of the Blueberry Pie ice cream flavor.

   O   O   The opinions of the owner and the head of marketing seem to be focused on finding a way to continue the Blueberry Pie ice cream flavor.

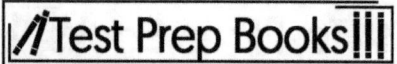

Practice Test #1

Prompt 2
A company has specific rules for paying employees premium pay (any time worked beyond the salaried 8-hour shift worked five days per week). The four types of premium pay and how they can be applied are described by the following excerpts.

Excerpt 1
Any employee who is scheduled to work any hours on a Sunday can claim Sunday differential. Sunday differential cannot be combined with any other type of premium pay, except night differential. Sunday differential is valued at 1.3 times an employee's base pay.

Excerpt 2
Night differential is offered in addition to regular base pay for time worked between the hours of 6:00 p.m. and 6:00 a.m. Night differential is valued at 1.25 times an employee's base pay.

Excerpt 3
Overtime is offered for hours worked beyond a regularly scheduled 8-hour shift that is worked five days per week. Overtime is valued at 1.5 times an employee's base pay.

Excerpt 4
Holiday pay is offered for hours, up to a maximum of 8 hours, that are worked on a federally designated holiday. Holiday pay cannot be combined with any other premium pay. Holiday pay is valued at two times an employee's base pay.

3. Based on the information provided, answer the following questions.

Yes   No

○   ○   An employee who works from 7:00 a.m. to 3:00 p.m. on July 4 (not falling on a Sunday) is eligible for 8 hours of premium pay.

○   ○   An employee who works from 5:00 a.m. to 3:00 p.m. on July 4 (not falling on a Sunday) is eligible for 10 hours of holiday pay.

4. Employee A works the following shifts:
- Sunday: 9:00 a.m. to 5:00 p.m.
- Monday: 12:00 p.m. to 8:00 p.m.
- Tuesday: is scheduled off, but picks up a shift from 10:00 a.m. to 6:00 p.m.
- Wednesday: 6:00 a.m. to 2:00 p.m.
- Thursday: 5:00 a.m. to 1:00 p.m.
- Friday: 3:00 p.m. to 11:00 p.m.

If none of these days are a holiday, what is the maximum possible hours of premium pay the employee is eligible to receive?
   a. 10 hours
   b. 12 hours
   c. 16 hours
   d. 21 hours
   e. 24 hours

Practice Test #1

Graphic Interpretation

5. The average decrease in price for every increase in demand per slice is:
   a. $0.25
   b. $0.50
   c. $0.125
   d. $0.75

The price per slice and the quantity demanded have a:
   a. positive correlation
   b. negative correlation
   c. no apparent correlation

6. The diagram below shows the organization of rational and irrational numbers. From this, it can be determined that all are rational numbers, except:
   a. 0
   b. $\sqrt{3}$
   c. $\frac{1}{3}$
   d. $-\frac{1}{3}$

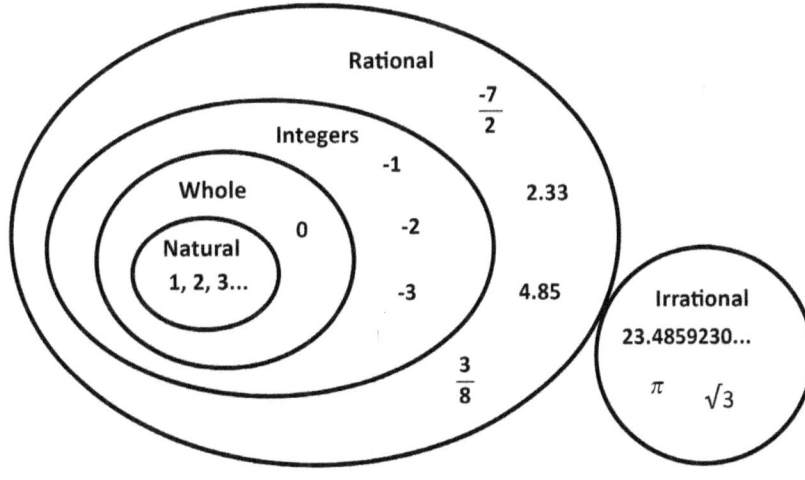

Real House Prices and Mortgage Rates

7. This graph shows the relation between real house prices and Freddie Mac Survey mortgage rates between January 1976 and January 2014.
This window of time maintains the largest consistent discrepancy between the real house prices and the survey house prices.

   a. January 1981–January 1983
   b. January 1980–January 1982
   c. January 1998–January 2000
   d. January 2006–January 2008

Practice Test #1

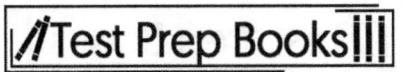

The real house price rises above the survey house price for the first time on approximately which date?
a. January 1995
b. January 1986
c. January 1989

Two-Part Analysis

8. Max can complete an analysis in 5 hours, while Dottie can compete the same analysis in 3 hours. Select a value for the time it would take them to finish the analysis if they worked together and by what difference this would be faster than Dottie's time.

Time Together	Difference	
O	O	1.625
O	O	1.875
O	O	1.125
O	O	0.625

9. Employees at Sales, Inc., must secure 10 sales per year. After their initial 10 sales, they receive an additional bonus of 5 percent of their base salary for every sale past the first 10 sales. For every sale over 20, an employee receives a bonus of $15,000 per sale. Employee A has a base salary of $54,000 and secures 12 sales. Employee B has a base salary of $62,000 and secures 21 sales. What equations could be used to calculate Employee B's pay and the difference between Employee A and Employee B's pay?

Employee B's Pay	Pay Difference Between Employee A and Employee B	
O	O	$54{,}000 + (a - 10)(0.05)(54{,}000)$
O	O	$62{,}000 + (b - 20)(15{,}000) + (b - 10)(0.05)(62{,}000)$
O	O	$54{,}000 + (a - 20)(15{,}000) + (a - 10)(.5)(54{,}000)$
O	O	$62{,}000 + (b - 20)(15{,}000) + (.05)(62{,}000)$
O	O	$62{,}000 + (b - 20)(15{,}000) + (b - 10)(0.05)(62{,}000)$ $- (54{,}000 + (a - 10)(0.05)(54{,}000))$

Table Analysis

Employee	Years	Position	Salary
Johnson	10	Warehouse	$44,000
Jones	15	HR	$45,000
Baker	19	Payroll	$42,000
Grande	9	Management	$81,000
Mays	4	Sales	$65,000
Innis	1	HR	$32,000
Richmond	6	Management	$92,000
Simpson	17	Marketing	$90,000
Douglas	22	HR	$50,000
Ryan	27	Warehouse	$49,000
Zimmers	2	Warehouse	$38,000

10.

TRUE	FALSE	
○	○	The average number of years in the warehouse division is 12 years.
○	○	The difference in average salary between the sales and management divisions is $21,500.
○	○	The division with the highest total number of years of experience in that position is the warehouse.

Practice Test #1

11.

TRUE	FALSE	
○	○	A plot of the years of experience versus salary would show a positive correlation.

Boys Game More Frequently

About how often do you play games?

	All teen gamers	Boy gamers	Girl gamers
Several times a day	13 %	19 %	6 %
About once a day	18	20	16
3 to 5 days a week	21	27	15
1 to 2 days a week	23	23	23
Every few weeks	15	7	23
Less often	10	4	17

12.

TRUE	FALSE	
○	○	The ratio of boy gamers to girl gamers who play about once a day is 5:4.
○	○	The percent of girl gamers compared to boy gamers in the categories of 3 to 5 days a week and 1 to 2 days a week is 72 percent.
○	○	The number of girl gamers tends to increase as the frequency of play during the week decreases.

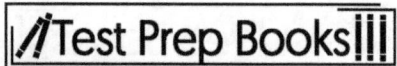

Data Sufficiency

Decide whether the data given in the statements are sufficient to answer the question.

13. A motorcycle race consists of three legs. On the first two legs of the race, a motorcycle travels an average of 50 miles per hour. On the last leg of the race, it travels an average of 75 miles per hour. What is this motorcycle's average speed for the entire race in miles per hour?

    1) All three legs are of equal length.

    2) The total distance is 450 miles.

    a. Statement (1) ALONE is sufficient, but statement (2) alone is not sufficient to answer the question asked.
    b. Statement (2) ALONE is sufficient, but statement (1) alone is not sufficient to answer the question asked.
    c. BOTH statements (1) and (2) TOGETHER are sufficient to answer the question asked, but NEITHER statement ALONE is sufficient to answer the question asked.
    d. EACH statement ALONE is sufficient to answer the question asked.
    e. Statements (1) and (2) TOGETHER are NOT sufficient to answer the question asked, and additional data specific to the problem are needed.

14. How many cans of paint can Jessica buy with $16?

    1) One color was $1 more per can than the other.

    2) She only bought red cans and blue cans, and she bought two more blue cans than red cans.

    a. Statement (1) ALONE is sufficient, but statement (2) alone is not sufficient to answer the question asked.
    b. Statement (2) ALONE is sufficient, but statement (1) alone is not sufficient to answer the question asked.
    c. BOTH statements (1) and (2) TOGETHER are sufficient to answer the question asked, but NEITHER statement ALONE is sufficient to answer the question asked.
    d. EACH statement ALONE is sufficient to answer the question asked.
    e. Statements (1) and (2) TOGETHER are NOT sufficient to answer the question asked, and additional data specific to the problem are needed.

15. Choose the correct statement(s) for the following equation: $\sqrt{x^2 - 2xy + y^2} = 16$

   1) $x > 0$

   2) $x = 5y$

   a. Statement (1) ALONE is sufficient, but statement (2) alone is not sufficient to answer the question asked.
   b. Statement (2) ALONE is sufficient, but statement (1) alone is not sufficient to answer the question asked.
   c. BOTH statements (1) and (2) TOGETHER are sufficient to answer the question asked, but NEITHER statement ALONE is sufficient to answer the question asked.
   d. EACH statement ALONE is sufficient to answer the question asked.
   e. Statements (1) and (2) TOGETHER are NOT sufficient to answer the question asked, and additional data specific to the problem are needed.

16. An employee receives 12 percent commission on every sale. How much was the sale price of sale x?

   1) Commission = $156

   2) Sale x + Sale y = $20,000

   a. Statement (1) ALONE is sufficient, but statement (2) alone is not sufficient to answer the question asked.
   b. Statement (2) ALONE is sufficient, but statement (1) alone is not sufficient to answer the question asked.
   c. BOTH statements (1) and (2) TOGETHER are sufficient to answer the question asked, but NEITHER statement ALONE is sufficient to answer the question asked.
   d. EACH statement ALONE is sufficient to answer the question asked.
   e. Statements (1) and (2) TOGETHER are NOT sufficient to answer the question asked, and additional data specific to the problem are needed.

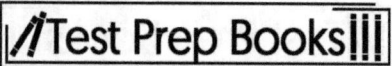

17. Of the 804 graduating seniors, a portion are going on to salaried positions after college. Approximately $\frac{1}{4}$ of those positions will be in state. What is the closest estimate for how many graduates taking salaried positions will be staying in state?

    1) $\frac{2}{5}$ of the 804 are going on to salaried positions.

    2) $\frac{3}{4}$ of the salaried positions are out of state.

    a. Statement (1) ALONE is sufficient, but statement (2) alone is not sufficient to answer the question asked.
    b. Statement (2) ALONE is sufficient, but statement (1) alone is not sufficient to answer the question asked.
    c. BOTH statements (1) and (2) TOGETHER are sufficient to answer the question asked, but NEITHER statement ALONE is sufficient to answer the question asked.
    d. EACH statement ALONE is sufficient to answer the question asked.
    e. Statements (1) and (2) TOGETHER are NOT sufficient to answer the question asked, and additional data specific to the problem are needed.

18. A bag contains red, blue, and white marbles. What are the chances a red marble is drawn out of a bag on the first try?

    1) The bag contains a total of 12 marbles.

    2) There is a $\frac{1}{2}$ chance of drawing a white marble and a $\frac{1}{4}$ chance of drawing a blue marble.

    a. Statement (1) ALONE is sufficient, but statement (2) alone is not sufficient to answer the question asked.
    b. Statement (2) ALONE is sufficient, but statement (1) alone is not sufficient to answer the question asked.
    c. BOTH statements (1) and (2) TOGETHER are sufficient to answer the question asked, but NEITHER statement ALONE is sufficient to answer the question asked.
    d. EACH statement ALONE is sufficient to answer the question asked.
    e. Statements (1) and (2) TOGETHER are NOT sufficient to answer the question asked, and additional data specific to the problem are needed.

19. A local deli offers customers a choice of meat, bread, and cheese for their sandwiches. How many different combinations are there for a sandwich selection?

   1) Wheat bread is the most popular choice of bread.

   2) There are three types of meat, three types of cheese, and five types of bread.

   a. Statement (1) ALONE is sufficient, but statement (2) alone is not sufficient to answer the question asked.
   b. Statement (2) ALONE is sufficient, but statement (1) alone is not sufficient to answer the question asked.
   c. BOTH statements (1) and (2) TOGETHER are sufficient to answer the question asked, but NEITHER statement ALONE is sufficient to answer the question asked.
   d. EACH statement ALONE is sufficient to answer the question asked.
   e. Statements (1) and (2) TOGETHER are NOT sufficient to answer the question asked, and additional data specific to the problem are needed.

20. What is 40 percent of 20w?

   1) $w \neq 0$

   2) w is positive

   a. Statement (1) ALONE is sufficient, but statement (2) alone is not sufficient to answer the question asked.
   b. Statement (2) ALONE is sufficient, but statement (1) alone is not sufficient to answer the question asked.
   c. BOTH statements (1) and (2) TOGETHER are sufficient to answer the question asked, but NEITHER statement ALONE is sufficient to answer the question asked.
   d. EACH statement ALONE is sufficient to answer the question asked.
   e. Statements (1) and (2) TOGETHER are NOT sufficient to answer the question asked, and additional data specific to the problem are needed.

Answer Explanations #1

Quantitative Reasoning

1. A: Compare each number after the decimal point to figure out which overall number is greatest. In Choices A (1.43785) and C (1.43592), both have the same tenths place (4) and hundredths place (3). However, the thousandths place is greater in Choice A (7), so A has the greatest value overall.

2. D: By rearranging and grouping the factors in Choice D, we can notice that $3 \times 3 \times 4 \times 2 = (3 \times 2) \times (4 \times 3) = 6 \times 12$, which is what we were looking for.

3. E: The new price of the purse can be found by first multiplying the original price by 25%, or 0.25. This yields an increase of $32. Taking the original price of $128 and adding the increase in price of $32 yields a new price of $160.

4. B: Since $850 is the price after a 20% discount, $850 represents 80% (or 0.8) of the original price. In other words, $850 = 0.8x$ (where x is the original price). Solving this, we find $x = \frac{850}{0.8} = 1,062.5$. Now, to find the savings, calculate the original price minus the sale price: $1,062.50 - \$850 = \$212.50$.

5. E: To find what 85% of 20 questions is, multiply 20 by .85:

$$20 \times .85 = 17 \text{ questions}$$

6. B: Using the conversion rate, multiply the projected weight loss of 25 lb by $0.45 \frac{kg}{lb}$ to get the amount in kilograms (11.25 kg).

7. D: First, subtract $1,437 from $2,334.50 to find Johnny's monthly savings; this equals $897.50. Then, multiply this amount by 3 to find out how much he will have (in 3 months) before he pays for his vacation; this equals $2,692.50. Finally, subtract the cost of the vacation ($1,750) from this amount to find how much Johnny will have left: $942.50.

8. B: Dividing by 98 can be approximated by dividing by 100, which would mean shifting the decimal point of the numerator to the left by 2. The result is 4.2, which rounds to 4.

9. D: To find the average of a set of values, add the values together and then divide by the total number of values. In this case, include the unknown value of what Dwayne needs to score on his next test, in order to solve it.

$$\frac{78 + 92 + 83 + 97 + x}{5} = 90$$

Then multiply each side by 5 to simplify the equation, resulting in:

$$78 + 92 + 83 + 97 + x = 450$$
$$350 + x = 450$$
$$x = 100$$

Dwayne would need to get a perfect score of 100 in order to get an average of at least 90.

Answer Explanations #1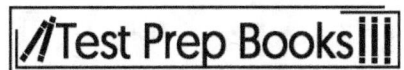

Test this answer by substituting back into the original formula.

$$\frac{78 + 92 + 83 + 97 + 100}{5} = 90$$

10. D: For an even number of total values, the median is calculated by finding the mean, or average, of the two middle values once all values have been arranged in ascending order from least to greatest. In this case, $(92 + 83) \div 2$ would equal the median 87.5, Choice *D*.

11. C: Follow the order of operations in order to solve this problem. Solve the parentheses first, following the order of operations inside the parentheses as well. First, simplify the square roots.

$$(6 \times 4) - 3^2$$

Then, multiply inside the parentheses:

$$24 - 3^2$$

Next, simplify the exponents:

$$24 - 9$$

Finally, subtract to get 15, Choice *C*.

12. D: Three girls for every two boys can be expressed as a ratio: $3:2$. This can be visualized as splitting the school into five groups: three girl groups and two boy groups. The number of students that are in each group can be found by dividing the total number of students by five:

$$\frac{650 \text{ students}}{5 \text{ groups}} = \frac{130 \text{ students}}{\text{group}}$$

To find the total number of girls, multiply the number of students per group (130) by the number of girl groups in the school (3). This equals 390, Choice *D*.

13. E: If the average of all six numbers is 6, that means

$$\frac{a + b + c + d + e + x}{6} = 6$$

The sum of the first five numbers is 25, so this equation can be simplified to:

$$\frac{25 + x}{6} = 6$$

Multiplying both sides by 6 gives $25 + x = 36$, and x, or the sixth number, can be solved to equal 11.

14. C: Kimberley worked 4.5 hours at the rate of \$10 / h and 1 hour at the rate of \$12 / h. The problem states that her time is rounded to the nearest hour, so the 4.5 hours would round up to 5 hours at the rate of \$10 / h.

$$(5 \text{ h}) \times \left(\frac{\$10}{\text{h}}\right) + (1 \text{ h}) \times \left(\frac{\$12}{\text{h}}\right) = \$50 + \$12 = \$62$$

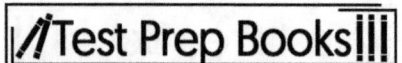

Answer Explanations #1

15. A: The cost of the jackets is $47 \times 2 = \$94$. The cost of the boots is $\$38 \times 3 = \$114$. The total cost is $\$94 + \$114 = \$208$. Choice *B* only accounted for the cost of the jackets and Choice *C* only accounted for the cost of the boots. Choice *D* had the number of jackets and boots mixed. Choice *E* only accounted for 2 jackets and 2 pairs of boots.

16. C: For each fraction, we can divide the numerator by the denominator to find a decimal value. $4/5 = 0.8$, $2/3 \approx 0.67$, and $91/100 = 0.91$. Ordering these from least to greatest gives us 0.67, 0.8, 0.85, and 0.91, which matches Choice *C*.

17. B: First, calculate the difference between the larger value and the smaller value.

$$378 - 252 = 126$$

This means that there was an increase of 126 customers. Next, find what percent of 252 this would be. To do this set 126 over 252.

$$\frac{126}{252} = .5$$

Now multiply by 100 to turn this into a percent.

$$0.5 \times 100 = 50\%$$

18. C: 40% of y is 24, so $0.4y = 24$. Dividing both sides of the equation by 0.4 results in $y = 60$. Also, it is true that $\frac{60}{120} = 0.5$, so 60 is 50% of 120. Therefore, the answer is 50%.

19. A: To find the fraction of the bill that the first three people pay, the fractions need to be added, which means finding the common denominator. The common denominator will be 60:

$$\frac{1}{5} + \frac{1}{4} + \frac{1}{3} = \frac{12}{60} + \frac{15}{60} + \frac{20}{60} = \frac{47}{60}$$

The remainder of the bill is:

$$1 - \frac{47}{60} = \frac{60}{60} - \frac{47}{60} = \frac{13}{60}$$

20. B: Simplify each mixed number of the problem into a fraction by multiplying the denominator by the whole number and adding the numerator:

$$\frac{14}{3} - \frac{31}{9}$$

Since the first denominator is a multiple of the second, simplify it further by multiplying both the numerator and denominator of the first expression by 3 so that the denominators of the fractions are equal.

$$\frac{42}{9} - \frac{31}{9} = \frac{11}{9}$$

Answer Explanations #1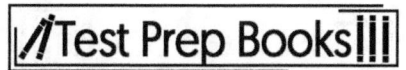

Simplifying this further, divide the numerator 11 by the denominator 9; this leaves 1 with a remainder of 2. To write this as a mixed number, place the remainder over the denominator, resulting in $1\frac{2}{9}$.

21. A: The total fraction taken up by green and red shirts will be:

$$\frac{1}{3} + \frac{2}{5} = \frac{5}{15} + \frac{6}{15} = \frac{11}{15}$$

The remaining fraction is:

$$1 - \frac{11}{15} = \frac{15}{15} - \frac{11}{15} = \frac{4}{15}$$

Verbal Reasoning

Reading Comprehension

1. C: Choice A is incorrect because the seaport is noted as "thriving." Choice B is incorrect because the slave traders actually built both office structures and slave holding buildings in downtown Alexandria; there is no mention of renting, or of landlords. Choice C is correct because Joseph Bruin bought hundreds of slaves during the years 1844 to 1861. Choice D is incorrect because the Bruin Slave Jail is stated as NOT open to the public. Choice E is incorrect because the passage notes that the offices and slave holding units were open until the end of the Civil War.

2. A: Choices B, C, D, and E can all be regarded as false based on the information provided in the passage. Choice A contains information provided in the passage; therefore, the statement is true. Choice B is false because the passage states that Joseph Bruin was imprisoned in 1861; it does not say that his business lasted until the end of the Civil War. Choice C is false because the slave pen was not four stories high; the passage specifically noted that the slave pen was two stories high. Choice D is false because the passage does not refer to Union or Confederate soldiers, and the Bruin Slave Jail was what became the Fairfax County courthouse. Choice E is false because there is no information in the passage that indicates that literature, like *Uncle Tom's Cabin*, was preserved by the Northern Virginia Urban League.

3. D: Choice A is false, based on the passage statement that Alexandria was founded in 1749. Choice B is false because the passage does not suggest that Harriet Beecher Stowe was a slave; rather, the passage states that Stowe was the author of *Uncle Tom's Cabin*. Choice C is incorrect; the passage states that northern abolitionists helped to save two slave sisters. Choice D is true based on the information found in the passage. Choice E is false; the town of Annapolis is not mentioned in the passage.

4. C: The purpose of the passage is to shed light on the history of Joseph Bruin's Slave Jail and what became of it. Choice A is incorrect because while the two sisters are mentioned in the story to provide details, they are not the main purpose of the story. Choice B is incorrect because while the beginning of the story contains the information about the town and its slave business, this answer option leaves out the fact that the passage is focused on one slave jail in particular and omits anything about the conclusion of the passage, which is actually key in the main focus of the passage—how Joseph Bruin's Slave Jail came about and what became of it. Choice D is incorrect because the point of the passage is not about where the historical Bruin Slave Jail currently stands but the history behind it.

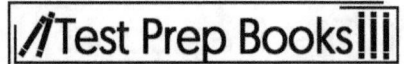

Answer Explanations #1

5. C: Because the details in Choice A and Choice B are examples of how an emotionally intelligent leader operates, they are not the best choice for the definition of the term *emotional intelligence*. They are qualities observed in an EI leader. Choice C explicitly states what EI means. Choice D does not directly relate to EI, and Choice E lists characteristics of an unsuccessful leader.

6. C: Choice E can be eliminated immediately because of the signal word "always." Choice A can be eliminated because it does not reflect an accurate fact. Choices B and D do not support claims about how to be a successful leader.

7. E: The qualities of an unsuccessful leader possessing a transactional leadership style are listed in the passage. Choices A and B are incorrect because these options reflect the qualities of a successful leader. Choices C and D are definitely not characteristics of a successful leader; however, they are not presented in the passage and readers should do their best to ignore such options.

8. D: Even though some choices may be true of successful leaders, the best answer must be supported by sub-points in the passage. Therefore, Choices A and C are incorrect. Choice B is incorrect because uncompromising transactional leadership styles squelch success. Choice E is never mentioned in the passage.

9. E: To support Choice E, the idea that a leader can develop emotional intelligence if desired, the passage says, "There are ways to develop emotional intelligence for the person who wants to improve their leadership style." After a careful reading of the passage about emotional intelligence, readers can select points for the statements that are contradictory in the selection. For example, the statement that contradicts Choice A says, "Becoming a successful leader in today's industry, government, and nonprofit sectors requires more than a high intelligence quotient (IQ)." Likewise, a contradictory passage for Choice C is: "Building relationships outside the institution with leadership coaches and with professional development trainers can also help leaders who want to grow their leadership success." Choices B and D do not have supporting evidence in the passage to make them true.

10. B: Readers should carefully focus their attention on the beginning of the passage to answer this series of questions. Even though the sentences may be worded a bit differently, all but one statement is true. It presents a false idea that descriptive details are not necessary until the climax of the story. Even if one does not read the passage, he or she probably knows that all good writing begins with descriptive details to develop the main theme the writer intends for the narrative.

11. C: Choice C allows room for the fact that not all people who attempt to write a play will find it easy. If the writer follows the basic principles of narrative writing described in the passage, however, writing a play does not have to be an excruciating experience. None of the other options can be supported by points from the passage.

12. C: Choice C is true based on the information that claims an image is like using a thousand words. Choice A is incorrect based on the sentence that reads, "Next, use dialogue to reveal the attitudes and personalities of each of the characters who have a key part in the unfolding story." Choice B is false because drama does not necessarily need to be predictable. Choice D contradicts the point that the protagonist should experience self-discovery. Finally, Choice E is incorrect because all drama suggests some challenge for the characters to experience.

13. B: To suggest that a 10 minute play is accessible does not imply any timeline, nor does the passage mention how long a playwright spends with revisions and rewrites. So, Choice A is incorrect. Choice B is

Answer Explanations #1

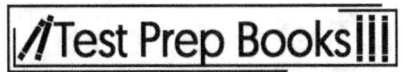

correct because of the opening statement that reads, "Learning how to write a 10 minute play may seem like a monumental task at first; but, if you follow a simple creative writing strategy, similar to the ones used for writing narrative stories, you will be able to write a successful drama. None of the remaining choices are supported by points in the passage.

14. E: Note that the only element not mentioned in the passage is the style feature that is part of a narrative writer's tool kit. It is not to say that 10 minute plays do not have style. The correct answer denotes only that the element of style was not illustrated in this particular passage.

Critical Reasoning

15. E: Choice A is incorrect. Alexis is not reinforcing Dalton's argument here because she offers no solidarity with his argument that agribusiness produces greenhouse emissions. Therefore, Choice A is incorrect.

Choice B is also incorrect. Alexis does not add to Dalton's argument in any way, because the foundation of the two arguments are fundamentally different.

Choice C is incorrect. It might be tempting to pick Choice C; however, it doesn't give us the whole picture. Alexis' response mostly gives an alternative viewpoint.

Choice D is incorrect. Similar to Choice B, Alexis does not offer any claims to back up Dalton's argument, though she does offer a claim to back up a differing argument.

Choice E is the best answer because Alexis is suggesting an alternative factor to the problem of global warming by offering a differing cause other than agribusiness, coupled with a differing solution.

Therefore, Choice E is the correct answer.

16. D: Choice A is incorrect. There is no evidence that the speaker thinks that Shelby is an excellent coder. They only indicate that she is "proficient." Eliminate this choice.

Choice B is incorrect. Shelby has fifteen years of experience, which serves as the speaker's evidence that she is a proficient coder, not that the company is looking for someone with fifteen years of experience.

Choice C is also incorrect. If anything, the speaker assumes that Shelby will be a good fit for the company, not a bad fit for the company. The speaker is recommending Shelby for the job.

Choice D is the best choice here. The speaker assumes that someone having fifteen years of experience will make them a proficient coder. Although this is quite possibly true, the speaker is still making an assumption about Shelby's skills.

Choice E is incorrect. The speaker has not compared Shelby to anyone else in their statement.

Therefore, Choice D is the correct answer.

17. B: Choice A is incorrect because it offers continued advice for those who agree with the statement.

Choice B is the correct answer choice. The speaker's argument says that everyone should eat meat because the only way to fulfill protein needs is from the complete protein in meat. However, if the statement were introduced into the argument that complete protein could be created in an alternative

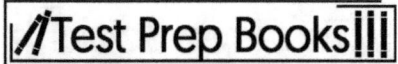

way than simply eating meat, it would weaken the speaker's original argument. Choice B is the best choice.

Choice C is incorrect. Facts about amino acids would not weaken the presented argument. This information acts as background context for the presented argument.

Choice D is misleading. The answer choice states that fruits and vegetables contain essential nutrients that help our bodies fight disease. This doesn't strengthen or weaken the original argument; it's a distractor.

Choice E is also a distractor, like Choice D. It doesn't strengthen or weaken the original argument, it just provides different information about nutrients.

Therefore, Choice B is the correct answer.

18. D: Choice A is irrelevant. The argument makes no mention as to when John works out. Would it weaken the conclusion—which is that years of gym time have clearly paid off—if he works out in the morning instead of the afternoon? No, of course not. Eliminate this choice.

Choice B preys on those who incorrectly identify the conclusion. Test takers who identify the first sentence as the conclusion will find this answer very appealing. If John is the size of an NFL linebacker, but linebackers are much smaller than professional bodybuilders, then John doesn't look like a professional linebacker. However, Choice B is irrelevant as to whether years of working out have paid off. Eliminate this choice.

Choice C actually strengthens the argument. If John weighed considerably less before working out and now he looks like a professional bodybuilder, then years of working out have definitely paid off. Eliminate this choice.

Choice D looks very appealing. If John's family members are all similar in size without weightlifting, then it's possible that it doesn't matter that John regularly spends time in the gym. Even without lifting, John would likely be the same size as his male family members. Therefore, years of working out would not be the reason why he looks like a professional bodybuilder. Don't be concerned that Choice D is unlikely in reality. If a question says something's true, then treat it as true. Keep this choice for now.

Choice E reinforces the argument's conclusion. The argument already states that John has gone to the gym for years. Whether he goes three, five, or seven times per week does not weaken the argument. Eliminate this choice.

Therefore, Choice D is the correct answer.

19. D: Choice A is irrelevant. The argument's conclusion is that Hank is a professional writer. The argument does not depend on whether Hank's agent is the best or worst in the business. Eliminate this choice.

Choice B seems fairly strong at first glance. It feels reasonable to say that being a professional writer requires representation. However, the argument would still be strong if being a professional writer did not require an agent. Hank would still be a professional writer. Eliminate this choice.

Answer Explanations #1

Choice C is irrelevant. Whether Hank is a professional writer does not depend on his reviews. Eliminate this choice.

Choice D is strong. Negate it to determine if the argument falls apart. If being a professional writer requires earning money, then Hank would not be a professional writer. The argument falls apart. This is almost definitely the correct answer.

Choice E is irrelevant. The argument does not attempt to tie Hank's professionalism with a word count. For the purposes of this argument, it does not matter if Hank writes ten or ten thousand words per day. Eliminate this choice.

Therefore, Choice D is the correct answer.

20. A: Choice A looks very strong. The argument devotes most of its time discussing Quillium's popularity and monetary value. It uses these facts to conclude that Quillium is the most effective drug in treating blood pressure. If the most lucrative and popular drugs are not necessarily the most effective, then it seriously weakens the argument. Leave this choice for now, and look at the other answer choices.

Choice B strengthens the argument. Moving through the screening process at record time supports the conclusion. It definitely does not weaken it. Eliminate this choice.

Choice C is irrelevant. Whether Giant Pharma gouges its customers does not affect the conclusion concerning the drug's effectiveness. Eliminate this choice.

Choice D is misleading. This choice would greatly weaken if the argument's conclusion were that Quillium is the reason for Giant Pharma's high valuation. However, this is only a premise. Choice D weakens this premise, but it does not weaken the argument as much as Choice A, which attacks the heart of the argument. Eliminate this choice.

Choice E is irrelevant. The argument's conclusion is that Quillium is the most effective drug for treating irregular blood pressure. Does it matter if Quillium has alternate applications? Of course not, so eliminate this choice.

Therefore, Choice A is the correct answer.

21. A: Choice A is very strong since it provides an alternate explanation for the high valuation other than Julia. If the Company released an extremely popular application, then the application is the real reason for the 10 million dollar valuation. Furthermore, this answer choice explicitly states that the application was released before Julia's hiring. Keep this choice for now.

Choice B is irrelevant. Whether investors are properly evaluating the Company's price does not affect Julia's role in that valuation. Eliminate this choice.

Choice C strengthens the argument. If Julia is an expert in her field, then her skills could have been the reason for the valuation. Investors could have factored in Julia's expertise in their valuation. It definitely does not weaken the argument. Eliminate this choice.

Choice D is another strong answer choice. If Julia only worked at Michael Scott Paperless Company for two weeks, then it is less likely that she's the reason for the 10 million dollar valuation. However, if she's

79

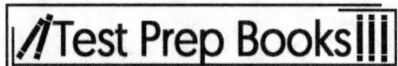

Answer Explanations #1

a renowned expert or extreme talent, then her hiring alone could have affected the valuation. This answer choice is less strong than Choice A, which provides a clear alternative explanation for the sudden increase in valuation. Since Choice A is stronger, eliminate Choice D.

Choice E strengthens the argument. If Julia completed two important projects during her first month, then she could very well be the reason for the valuation. It definitely does not weaken the argument; eliminate Choice E as well.

Therefore, Choice A is the correct answer.

22. C: Choice A does not identify a flaw in the advertisement's reasoning. The advertisement connects smoking with fatal disease. At no point does the advertisement confuse the cause and effect. Eliminate this choice.

Choice B is incorrect. The advertisement does not make any overly broad generalizations. Eliminate this choice.

Choice C correctly identifies the argument's flaw. The argument analogizes secondhand smoke with a gas chamber without offering any evidence concerning secondhand smoke's health risk. The advertisement is clearly relying on hyperbole. The advertisement's argument properly justifies smoking with adverse health effects, but it does not do the same for secondhand smoke. This is most likely the correct answer.

Choice D is incorrect. Nothing in the argument states that there's real dispute over smoking's effect on health. Eliminate this choice.

Choice E is not present in the argument. Eliminate this choice.

23. D: Choice A is true. According to the argument, all of the employees must complete a mandatory class on insider trading. Jake is an employee. Therefore, he must have taken a class on insider trading. Eliminate this choice.

Choice B is not necessarily true; however, it could be true. According to the argument, some employees must pass a certification course, but it does not mention whether Jake is one of those employees. This choice may or may not be true, so it cannot be the correct answer. Eliminate this choice.

Choice C restates a premise, so it is true. Therefore, it is incorrect for the purposes of this question. Eliminate this choice.

Choice D must be incorrect according to the argument. As previously discussed, all of the employees must take a class on insider trading. Jake is an employee, so he must have taken the class. Therefore, Choice D must not be true.

Choice E could be true. The argument states that investment banks hire dozens of lawyers. It does not mention whether any investment bank has ever been charged. Since this choice could be true, it's not the correct answer. Eliminate this choice.

Therefore, Choice D is the correct answer.

Answer Explanations #1

Data Insights

Multi-Source Reasoning

1. YES: All three communications are concentrated on the continuance of the Blueberry Pie ice cream flavor, by the focus on how the flavor is progressing and what future options there are for the flavor, whether a year-round flavor, a seasonal flavor, etc.

NO: There is no statement to elude to or confirm that the Blueberry Pie ice cream flavor was one of the company's original flavors.

NO: While it is stated that the Blueberry Pie flavor is a great seller, it doesn't give an indication as to the exact ranking of the flavor.

2. YES: All given communications focus on the future of the Blueberry Pie ice cream flavor. With the production cost changing, it will clearly be a topic covered in the next meeting.

YES: Both offer suggestions for adapting to the changes in production costs to continue the flavor.

3. YES: July 4 is a designated federal holiday, and an employee who works an 8-hour shift on that date is eligible for 8 hours of holiday pay.

NO: July 4 is a designated federal holiday, but an employee can only earn a maximum of 8 hours of holiday pay per holiday. The additional 2 hours would need to be classified as overtime.

4. E: See breakdown of maximum possible hours of premium pay.

- Sunday: 8 hours of Sunday differential
- Monday: 6 hours of regular pay + 2 hours of night differential
- Tuesday: 8 hours of overtime
- Wednesday: 8 hours of regular pay
- Thursday: 1 hour of night differential + 7 hours of regular pay
- Friday: 3 hours of regular pay + 5 hours of night differential
- Ignoring the hours of regular pay, $8 + 2 + 8 + 1 + 5 = 24$

Graphic Interpretation

5. A: This can be determined by calculating the slope of the line at any point or over the entire graph.

$$\frac{1.00 - 3.00}{9 - 1} = \frac{-2}{8} = \frac{-1}{4} = -0.25$$

The slope is -.25. This means that there is a $.25 decrease in cost per slice for every additional slice demanded.

B: A negative correlation shows a steady decrease in the values of the *y* (vertical) axis as the *x* (horizontal) axis increases. Choice *A* would show a steady increase in the *y*-axis values with a steady increase in the *x*-axis values, and Choice *C* would not show any apparent pattern.

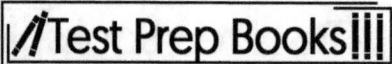

Answer Explanations #1

6. B: Since this choice has an irrational portion of $\sqrt{3}$, it would be classified as an irrational number. Choice A is a whole number, C is a rational fraction or repeating decimal, and D is the negative version of C.

7. D: While all choices (A, B, C, and D) contain large spikes in discrepancies between the real house prices and the survey house prices, January 2006 to January 2008 covers the largest window of discrepancies.

C: If you follow the line of survey house prices, it is below the real house price until approximately January of 1989 on the chart.

Two-Part Analysis

8. Time together = 1.875; Difference = 1.125

The method of calculating their combined analysis time is as follows:

$$\frac{1}{5} + \frac{1}{3} = \frac{1}{x}$$

$$\frac{15x}{1}\left(\frac{1}{5} + \frac{1}{3}\right) = \frac{15x}{1}\left(\frac{1}{x}\right)$$

$$3x + 5x = 15$$

$$8x = 15$$

$$x = \frac{15}{8} = 1.875$$

The difference would be calculated as follows:

$$3 - 1.875 = 1.125$$

All other choices are miscalculations of the rate or difference, particularly substituting in the wrong given rates.

9. Employee B's pay = $62,000 + (b - 20)(15,000) + (b - 10)(0.05)(62,000)$

This calculates the base pay plus any bonus over 20 sales plus the bonus for sales over 10.

Pay difference between A and B = $62,000 + (b - 20)(15,000) + (b - 10)(0.05)(62,000) - (54,000 + (a - 10)(0.05)(54,000))$

Other choices are miscalculations using the wrong adjustment for percentages or utilizing the wrong base salaries.

Answer Explanations #1

Table Analysis

10. FALSE: The average number of years is 13; the calculation is as follows:

$$\frac{10 + 27 + 2}{3} = 13$$

TRUE: The calculation is as follows:

Management salary average:

$$\frac{81,000 + 92,000}{2} = 86,500$$

Sales salary average:

$$\frac{65,000}{1} = 65,000$$

Difference = 86,500 − 65,000 = 21,500

TRUE: Addition of the total years for each department shows:

- HR = 38
- Warehouse = 39
- Marketing = 17
- Sales = 4
- Payroll = 19
- Management = 15

11. FALSE: A plot of the points would show that there is no real correlation between years of experience and salary.

12. TRUE: Numbers from the chart show boy gamers to girl gamers = 20:16, reduced to 5:4.

FALSE: The calculation of this percent is as follows:

Boy gamers $27 + 23 = 50$

Girl gamers $15 + 23 = 38$

$38 = 50x$

$x = 0.76 = 76 \; percent$

TRUE: A plot of the number of girl gamers versus the number of times played per week would show the number increasing as the number of times played per week decreased.

13. A: Knowing that all three legs are equal is enough to solve the problem. If you let x represent the length of each leg, then the total length of the race becomes:

$$x + x + x = 3x$$

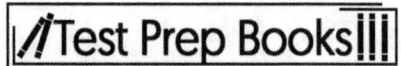

Answer Explanations #1

Then the time for each leg is the distance for each leg divided by the speed. Then getting like denominators gives:

$$\frac{3x}{150} + \frac{3x}{150} + \frac{2x}{150} = \frac{8x}{150}$$

Then, the average speed calculation is total distance over total time. So, you end up with:

$$\frac{3x}{\left(\frac{8x}{150}\right)}$$

Then solve from here:

$$3x \times \frac{150}{8x}$$

Cancel the x:

$$3 \times \frac{150}{8}$$

$$\frac{450}{8} = 56.25$$

Statement 2 is not sufficient because knowing the total length does not tell you what distances were traversed at 75 mph or 50 mph, so the time elapsed and thus average speed cannot be solved from the total distance alone.

14. E: Neither statement, even when taken together, provide enough information to answer the question. We need two equations to be able to set up simultaneous equations to solve together since we have two variables (the number of cans of red paint and the number of cans of blue paint). With statement 1, we are only told that one of the colors was $1 more than the other, but since we aren't told which is more expensive, we cannot form an equation that puts both colors in terms of the same variable. Similarly, with statement 2, we are only told she bought two more blue cans than red ones. Did she buy 1 red can and 3 blue? 2 red and 4 blue? 3 red and 5 blue? All we know is she bought at least 3 cans since she bought two more blue cans than red cans.

Because we don't even know exactly how much of the $16 she spent (she might have received change back), we can't work backwards and try plugging in numbers to try and see what numbers work out evenly. Moreover, we aren't told that the cans sell for an even dollar amount, just that one is $1 more than another. Perhaps one color is $1.50 and then the other is $2.50. Likewise, it's possible that one color is $2.10 and the other is $3.10. The possibilities are vast. There is not enough information to solve the problem.

Answer Explanations #1

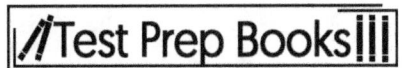

15. C: Both statements are necessary for completing the calculations as follows:

If $x > 0$, then 5y will also be > 0.

Factor the equation into $\sqrt{(x - y)^2} = 16$.

Then, take the square root of both sides and substitute $x = 5y$.

$$5y - y = 4$$

Therefore, $4y = 4$, so $y = 1$. Because the second statement says that $x = 5y$, $x = 5$.

16. A: Statement 1 is the only information necessary to complete the calculation as follows:

$$12 \; percent = 0.12$$
$$156 = 0.12x$$
$$x = \$1,300$$

17. A: Only statement 1 has information necessary to complete the calculations as follows:

$$\frac{2}{5}(804) = 321.6$$

$$\frac{1}{4}(321.6) = 80.4$$

$$80 \; positions$$

18. B: Only Statement 2 is necessary to calculate the solution as follows:

It's not necessary to know how many marbles there are in total since only one red marble is drawn from the bag of three colors. Statement 2 says that there is a $\frac{1}{2}$ chance of drawing a white marble and a $\frac{1}{4}$ chance of drawing a blue marble. Therefore, there is a $\frac{1}{4}$ chance of drawing a red marble since the sum of these fractions must equal 1.

19. B: Statement 1 contains frivolous information, but statement 2 contains information necessary to complete the calculation as follows:

3 meats × 3 cheeses × 5 breads = 45 choices for sandwiches

20. A: To calculate a value, statement 1 must be established to determine the answer is not 0. The information in statement 2 is not necessary to complete the solution.

Calculation is as follows:

$$40 \; percent = 0.40$$

$$0.40(20w) = 8w$$

Practice Test #2

Quantitative Reasoning

Problem Solving

1. Simplify:
$$\frac{4a^{-1}b^3}{a^4b^{-2}} \times \frac{3a}{b}$$

   a. $12a^3b^5$
   b. $12\frac{b^4}{a^4}$
   c. $\frac{12}{a^4}$
   d. $7\frac{b^4}{a}$
   e. $4\frac{7b}{a}$

2. What is the product of two irrational numbers?
   a. Irrational
   b. Rational
   c. Contradictory
   d. Complex and imaginary
   e. Irrational or rational

3. The number –4 can be classified as which of the following?
   a. Real, rational, integer, whole, natural
   b. Real, rational, integer, natural
   c. Real, rational, integer
   d. Real, irrational, complex
   e. Real, irrational, whole

4. If $n = 2^2$, and $m = n^2$, then m^n equals:
   a. 2^{12}
   b. 2^{10}
   c. 2^{18}
   d. 2^{16}
   e. 2^{20}

5. If $3x - 4 + 5x = 8 - 10x$, what is the value of x?
   a. 6
   b. -6
   c. 0.5
   d. 1.33
   e. 0.67

Practice Test #2

6. What are the zeros of the function: $f(x) = x^3 + 4x^2 + 4x$?
   a. -2
   b. 0, -2
   c. 2
   d. 0, 2
   e. 0, 0

7. If $g(x) = x^3 - 3x^2 - 2x + 6$ and $f(x) = 2$, then what is $g(f(x))$?
   a. -26
   b. 6
   c. $2x^3 - 6x^2 - 4x + 12$
   d. -2
   e. $2x^2 + 3x + 6$

8. What is the solution to the following system of equations?
$$x^2 - 2x + y = 8$$
$$x - y = -2$$
   a. $(-2, 3)$
   b. There is no solution.
   c. $(-2, 0) (1, 3)$
   d. $(-2, 0) (3, 5)$
   e. $(-2, 3) (3, 5)$

9. Which of the following shows the correct result of simplifying the following expression?
$$(7n + 3n^3 + 3) + (8n + 5n^3 + 2n^4)$$
   a. $9n^4 + 15n - 2$
   b. $2n^4 + 5n^3 + 15n - 2$
   c. $9n^4 + 8n^3 + 15n$
   d. $2n^4 + 8n^3 + 15n + 3$
   e. $3n^4 + 4n^3 + 15n - 4$

10. What is the product of the following expression?
$$(4x - 8)(5x^2 + x + 6)$$
   a. $20x^3 - 36x^2 + 16x - 48$
   b. $6x^3 - 41x^2 + 12x + 15$
   c. $20x^4 + 11x^2 - 37x - 12$
   d. $2x^3 - 11x^2 - 32x + 20$
   e. $10x^3 + 2x^2 - 8x + 48$

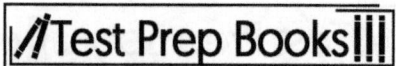

11. How could the following equation be factored to find the zeros?

$$y = x^3 - 3x^2 - 4x$$

a. $0 = x^2(x - 4), x = 0, 4$
b. $0 = 3x(x + 1)(x + 4), x = 0, -1, -4$
c. $0 = x(x + 1)(x + 6), x = 0, -1, -6$
d. $0 = x^2(x - 1)(x - 4), x = 0, -1, 4$
e. $0 = x(x + 1)(x - 4), x = 0, -1, 4$

12. What is the simplified quotient of $\frac{5x^3}{3x^2y} \div \frac{25}{3y^9}$?

a. $\frac{125x}{9y^{10}}$

b. $\frac{x}{5y^8}$

c. $\frac{5}{xy^8}$

d. $\frac{xy^8}{5}$

e. $\frac{xy^2}{5}$

13. What is the solution for the following equation?

$$\frac{x^2 + x - 30}{x - 5} = 11$$

a. $x = -6$
b. There is no solution.
c. $x = 16$
d. $x = 5$
e. $x = 6$

14. Mom's car drove 72 miles in 90 minutes. How fast did she drive in feet per second?
a. 0.8 feet per second
b. 48.9 feet per second
c. 0.009 feet per second
d. 70.4 feet per second
e. 55 feet per second

15. How do you solve $V = lwh$ for h?
    a. $lwV = h$
    b. $h = \frac{V}{lw}$
    c. $h = \frac{Vl}{w}$
    d. $h = \frac{Vw}{l}$
    e. $h = \frac{wl}{V}$

16. What is the domain for the function $y = \sqrt{x}$?
    a. All real numbers
    b. $x \geq 0$
    c. $x > 0$
    d. $y \geq 0$
    e. $y < 0$

17. If Sarah reads at an average rate of 21 pages in four nights, how long will it take her to read 140 pages?
    a. 6 nights
    b. 26 nights
    c. 8 nights
    d. 12 nights
    e. 27 nights

18. The phone bill is calculated each month using the equation $c = 50g + 75$. The cost of the phone bill per month is represented by c, and g represents the gigabytes of data used that month. What is the value and interpretation of the slope of this equation?
    a. 75 dollars per day
    b. 75 gigabytes per day
    c. 50 dollars per day
    d. 50 dollars per gigabyte
    e. 25 dollars per day

19. The ratio of fruit to vegetables at a grocery store is $5:3$. If the total number of produce items (fruits and vegetables) is 120, how many vegetables are in the store?
    a. 45
    b. 75
    c. 100
    d. 50
    e. 30

20. Katie ran 18 miles in 4 hours. Her rate in miles per hour is equivalent to which of the following proportions?
   a. 4 to 36
   b. 36 to 8
   c. 9 to 4
   d. 180 to 20
   e. 4 to 9

21. If $\sqrt[3]{m} = 2$ and $m = \sqrt{n}$, what is the value of n?
   a. 36
   b. 2
   c. 16
   d. 8
   e. 64

Verbal Reasoning

Reading Comprehension

Questions 1–4 are based on the following passage:

> A study by the Organization for Economic Development and Cooperation of ten developing countries during the period from 1985 to 1992 found significant implementation of privatization in only three countries. The study concluded that "reductions in the central budget deficit can only be marginal" because the impact was not evaluated over several years to consider the effect of the revenues forgone from state-owned enterprises (SOEs). Several later studies measured the budgetary effects and reported significant increases in profitability and productivity as a result of privatization, but the methodological flaws related to the difficulty of isolating the performance of SOEs from other elements rendered the findings ambiguous. While the evidence on the performance of SOEs "shows that state ownership is often correlated with politicization, inefficiency, and waste of resources," the assumption that it is state ownership that creates an environment influencing the quality of performance is not proven, with the empirical research on this point having yielded conflicting results. Given the inconclusive evidence, many scholars did not concur with a World Bank statement in 1995 that SOEs "remain an important obstacle to better economic performance."
>
> Reflecting a belief that the market is the best allocator of resources, experts have often recommended "unleashing" the private sector by removing regulations and privatizing SOEs. In 1995, to preclude hasty and simplistic privatization efforts, the World Bank recommended that SOEs be corporatized under commercial law and issued guidance on "[p]re-privatization interim measures and institutional arrangements for 'permanent SOEs.'" The bank also listed five preconditions for successful privatization: hard budget constraints; capital and labor market discipline; competition; corporate governance free of political interference; and commitment to privatization.

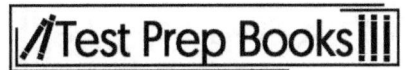

In view of the pervasive presence of SOEs in the global economy and their embodiment of political and economic considerations, SOEs are an entity to be considered and managed in the pursuit of stability.

"The State-Owned Enterprise as a Vehicle for Stability" by Neil Efird (2010), published by the Strategic Studies Institute (Department of Defense), pgs. 7–8

1. The World Bank stated which of the following in 1995?
    a. State-owned enterprises cannot impede economic performance.
    b. State-owned enterprises play a critical role in developing countries.
    c. State-owned enterprises promote economic and political stability.
    d. State-owned enterprises should be corporatized under commercial law gradually.
    e. State-owned enterprises might be inefficient, but the evidence is inconclusive.

2. Based on the passage above, which statement can be properly inferred?
    a. State-owned enterprises always cause economic stagnation.
    b. Privatization is controversial, even among economic experts.
    c. Economic studies are always subject to intense criticism and secondhand guessing.
    d. State-owned enterprises violate commercial law.
    e. The World Bank holds the power to directly intervene in economies.

3. Which statement(s) about state-owned enterprises are true based on the passage above?
    a. The empirical research demonstrates that state-owned enterprises are efficient and productive.
    b. Developing countries have little influence on the World Bank's policies.
    c. Privatization enjoys widespread popular support wherever it is implemented.
    d. State-owned enterprises do not have sizable effects on the global economy.
    e. According to the World Bank, successful privatization requires competition and corporate governance that is free of political interference, among other factors.

4. Which statement most accurately identifies the author's ultimate conclusion?
    a. The market is the best allocator of resources, so private enterprises will always outperform state-owned enterprises.
    b. The World Bank holds considerable expertise in matters related to state-owned enterprises and privatization.
    c. State-owned enterprises should be managed in a way that promotes economic stability, which might require a measured approach to privatization.
    d. Studies conducted with a flawed methodology should not be the basis for economic decisions.
    e. State-owned enterprises should be privatized under commercial law as long as the government adheres to the five preconditions for privatization.

Questions 5–8 are based on the following passage:

Scholars who have examined how national leaders historically craft public speeches in response to accusations of offensive words or deeds conclude that such officials generally rely upon one of two recurrent strategic approaches. The first of these is apologia, which William Benoit and Susan Brinson define as "a recurring type of discourse designed to restore face, image, or reputation after an alleged or suspected wrongdoing," which occurs during many apologies. The second is reconciliation, which John Hatch defines as "a dialogic rhetorical process of healing between the parties."

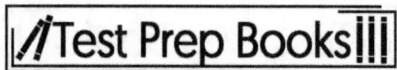

Speakers using apologia strive to restore their own credibility and remove any perception they might be guilty of involvement in the transgression. Speakers seeking reconciliation are interested in restoring dialogue instead of pursuing the purposes of shifting blame, denying charges, or some other form of blame avoidance or image repair.

Apologia focuses on short-term gains achievable by regaining favor with audiences already predisposed to the speaker's arguments. Reconciliation, by contrast, has a goal of understanding the long-term processes of image restoration and mutual respect between the aggrieved and the transgressor. Attempts at credible reconciliation utilize symbols of reunion to demonstrate that the aggrieved has *genuinely* granted the forgiveness sought by the offender. Visual images freeze the moment of genuine forgiveness and, when replayed in the online environment, carry forward the steps of reunification into perpetuity.

Not all offending images circulating in the online environment warrant a visual response or even an apology by national leaders. Nevertheless, failure to respond to the small number of potent images of transgressions that share characteristics qualifying them for continued recirculation in future propaganda efforts could be a costly mistake. Reconciliation provides a fruitful choice, as

its long-term goals match the ongoing need to handle ever-circulating images that offend.

Visual Propaganda and Extremism in the Online Environment, edited by Carol K. Winkler and Cori E. Dauber (2014), published by the Strategic Studies Institute (Department of Defense), "Visual Reconciliation as Strategy of Response to Offending Images" by Carol K. Winkler, excerpted from pages 63-64, 71-72, and 74

5. Which statement(s) accurately describe the difference between apologia and reconciliation based on the passage?
   a. Apologia is a dialogic rhetorical process that involves healing, while reconciliation seeks to restore the image of a party suspected of wrongdoing.
   b. Reconciliation utilizes symbols to demonstrate forgiveness, while apologia is always delivered in writing.
   c. Apologia is more effective in the short term, while reconciliation is more useful for improving relationships in the long term.
   d. Reconciliation seeks to close channels of communication, while apologia is more closely related to shifting blame and rehabilitating credibility.
   e. Apologia requires the aggrieved party's forgiveness, while reconciliation is a strategic approach to delivering visual responses.

6. Based on the passage above, which statement(s) can be properly inferred?
   a. National leaders should never apologize because reconciliation is always the superior option.
   b. Reconciliation is more effective than apologia because it is not self-serving.
   c. Apologia and reconciliation are most effective when delivered together.
   d. Apologia and reconciliation only function properly in the online environment.
   e. Maintaining a positive national image is an important part of governance.

7. Which statement(s) describe a feature of reconciliation?
   a. Reconciliation involves restoring dialogue and repairing relationships in the short term.
   b. Reconciliation leverages symbols of reunion to demonstrate that the aggrieved has genuinely granted the forgiveness sought by the offender.
   c. Reconciliation focuses on shifting blame, denying charges, restoring credibility, or otherwise repairing the offender's image.
   d. Reconciliation should be used when the audience is already predisposed to the speaker's argument.
   e. Reconciliation prioritizes short-term gains over substantively altering the underlying relationship.

8. Which statement(s) describes how the author believes national leaders should respond to offending images circulating in the online environment?
   a. National leaders should censor all offending images and attack any group that disseminates propaganda.
   b. National leaders should conduct an anti-propaganda campaign to raise public awareness about the dangers of sensationalism.
   c. The circulation of offending images in online environments is inevitable but relatively harmless, so this phenomenon should be ignored.
   d. All offending images should be addressed with either apologia or reconciliation, depending on which is more appropriate based on context.
   e. Some offending images do not warrant any response, but for the ones that do, reconciliation is the more appealing option due to its long-term impact.

Questions 9–11 are based on the following passage:

Despite spending far more on health care than any other nation, the United States ranks near the bottom on key health indicators. This paradox has been attributed to underinvestment in addressing social and behavioral determinants of health. A recent Institute of Medicine (IOM) report linked the shorter overall life expectancy in the United States to problems that are either caused by behavioral risks (e.g., injuries and homicides, adolescent pregnancy and sexually transmitted infections (STIs), HIV/AIDS, drug-related deaths, lung diseases, obesity, and diabetes) or affected by social conditions (e.g., birth outcomes, heart disease, and disability).

While spending more than other countries per capita on health care services, the United States spends less on average than do other nations on social services impacting social and behavioral determinants of health. Bradley, et al., found that Organization for Economic Co-operation and Development (OECD) nations with a higher ratio of spending on social services relative to health care services have better health and longer life expectancies than do those like the United States that have a lower ratio.

The Clinical & Translational Science Awards (CTSAs) established by the National Institutes of Health (NIH) have helped initiate interdisciplinary programs in more than sixty institutions that aim to advance the translation of research findings from "bench" to "bedside" to "community." Social and behavioral issues are inherent aspects of the translation of findings at the bench into better care and better health. Insofar as Clinical and Translational Science Institutes (CTSIs) will be evaluated for renewal—not only on the basis of their bench science discoveries, but also by their ability to move these discoveries into practice and improve individual and population health—the CTSIs should be motivated to include social and behavioral scientists in their work.

Population Health: Behavioral and Social Science Insights, Robert M. Kaplan et al. (2015), published by the Agency for Healthcare Research and Quality (National Institutes of Health), "Determinants of Health and Longevity" by Nancy E. Adler and Aric A. Prather, excerpted from pages 411 and 417

9. Which statement(s) describes how the United States differs in its approach to health care compared with other nations?
   a. On average, the United States spends more on social services impacting social and behavioral determinants of health than other nations.
   b. Compared with other nations, the United States has a higher ratio of spending on social services relative to health care services.
   c. Compared with other nations, the United States spends more per capita on health care services despite producing worse health outcomes.
   d. Compared with other nations, the United States has a lower life expectancy due to its lack of spending on health care services.
   e. Unlike other nations, the United States doesn't fund interdisciplinary programs that include behavioral and social science.

10. Based on the passage, which statement(s) describes the primary purpose of the Clinical and Translational Science Awards?
    a. The Clinical and Translational Science Awards advocate for the expansion of social services in the United States.
    b. The Clinical and Translational Science Awards seek to advance the translation of research findings from "bench" to "bedside" to "community."
    c. The Clinical and Translational Science Awards conduct research on how to mitigate the behavioral risks that have caused the decline in Americans' life expectancy.
    d. The Clinical and Translational Science Awards exclusively employ social and behavioral scientists, filling a void in the American health care system.
    e. The Clinical and Translational Science Awards calculate the optimal ratio for spending on social services relative to health care services.

11. Which statement(s) most accurately identifies the author's main thesis?
    a. Despite outspending other countries on health care, the United States performs poorly on key health indicators.
    b. The National Institutes of Health created the Clinical and Translational Science Awards to develop interdisciplinary programs in more than sixty institutions.
    c. Social and behavioral factors are an underappreciated aspect of health, and if they are better understood and properly addressed, health outcomes will improve.
    d. The United States has the shortest overall life expectancy in the world due to unaddressed behavioral risks and deteriorating social conditions.
    e. Life expectancy is the most important health care indicator because it encapsulates every other relevant factor.

Questions 12–14 are based on the following passages.

Passage I

Lethal force, or deadly force, is defined as the physical means to cause death or serious harm to another individual. The law holds that lethal force is only acceptable when you or another person are in immediate and unavoidable danger of death or severe bodily harm. For example, a person could be beating someone in such a way that the victim is suffering severe trauma that could result in death or serious harm. This would be an instance where lethal force would be acceptable and possibly the only way to save the victim from irrevocable damage.

Another example of when to use lethal force would be when someone enters your home with a deadly weapon. The intruder's presence and possession of the weapon indicate malicious intent and the ability to inflict death or severe injury upon you and your loved ones. Again, lethal force can be used in this situation. Lethal force can also be applied to prevent the harm of another individual. If a woman is being brutally assaulted and is unable to fend off an attacker, lethal force can be used to defend her as a last-ditch effort. If she is in immediate jeopardy of rape, harm, and/or death, lethal force could be the only response that could effectively deter the assailant.

The key to understanding the concept of lethal force is the term *last resort*. Deadly force cannot be taken back; it should be used only to prevent severe harm or death. The law does distinguish whether the means of one's self-defense is fully warranted or if the individual goes out of control in the process. If you continually attack the assailant after they are rendered incapacitated, this would be causing unnecessary harm, and the law can bring charges against you. Likewise, if you kill an attacker unnecessarily after defending yourself, you can be charged with murder. This would move lethal force beyond necessary defense, making it no longer a last resort but rather a use of excessive force.

Passage II

Assault is an unlawful and intentional act that causes reasonable apprehension in another individual, either by an imminent threat or by initiating offensive contact. Assaults can vary, encompassing physical strikes, threatening body language, and even provocative language. In the case of the latter, even if a hand has not been laid, it is still considered an assault because of its threatening nature.

Let's look at an example. A homeowner is angered because his neighbor blows fallen leaves onto his freshly mowed lawn. Irate, the homeowner gestures a fist to his neighbor and threatens to bash his head in for littering on his lawn. The homeowner's physical motions and verbal threats herald a physical threat against the other neighbor. These factors classify the homeowner's reaction as an assault. If the angry neighbor hits the threatening homeowner in retaliation, that would constitute an assault as well because he physically hit the homeowner.

Assault also centers on the involvement of weapons in a conflict. If someone fired a gun at another person, it could be interpreted as an assault, unless the shooter acted in self-defense. If an individual drew a gun or a knife on someone with the intent to harm them, it would be considered assault. However, it's also considered an assault if someone simply aims a weapon, loaded or not, at another person in a threatening manner.

12. The purpose of the second passage is to:
    a. To inform the reader about what assault is and how it is committed
    b. To inform the reader about how assault is a minor example of lethal force
    c. To disprove the previous passage concerning lethal force
    d. To argue that the use of assault is more common than the use of lethal force
    e. To recount an incident in which the author was assaulted

13. Given the information in the passages, one true thing about assault is that:
    a. All assault is considered an expression of lethal force.
    b. There are various forms of assault.
    c. Smaller, weaker people cannot commit assault.
    d. Assault is justified only as a last resort.
    e. Assault charges are more severe than unnecessary use of force charges.

14. The way in which the passages are structured is that:
    a. Both passages open by defining a legal concept and then continue to describe situations in order to further explain the concept.
    b. Both passages begin with situations, introduce accepted definitions, and then cite legal ramifications.
    c. The first passage presents a long definition while the second passage begins by showing an example of assault.
    d. Both cite specific legal doctrines and proceed to explain the rulings.
    e. The first passage explains both concepts and then focuses on lethal force. The second passage picks up with assault and explains the concept in depth.

Critical Reasoning

15. Teacher: Students don't need parental involvement to succeed. In my class of twenty kids, the two highest achieving students come from foster homes. There are too many children in the foster homes for their parents to monitor homework and enforce study habits. It's always the case that students can overcome their parents' indifference.
What mistake does the teacher commit in his reasoning?
    a. The teacher incorrectly applies a common rule.
    b. The teacher's conclusion is totally unjustified.
    c. The teacher relies on an unreasonably small sample size in drawing his conclusion.
    d. The teacher fails to consider competing theories.
    e. The teacher is biased.

16. Trent is a member of the SWAT Team, the most elite tactical unit at the city's police department. SWAT apprehends more suspected criminals than all other police units combined. Taken as a whole, the police department solves a higher percentage of crime than ever before in its history. Within the SWAT team, Trent's four-man unit is the most successful. However, the number of unsolved crime increases every year.
Which of the following statements, if true, most logically resolves the apparent paradox?
    a. Trent's SWAT team is the city's best police unit.
    b. Violent crime has decreased dramatically, while petty drug offenses have increased substantially.
    c. The total number of crimes increases every year.
    d. Aside from the SWAT units, the police department is largely incompetent.
    e. The police department focuses more on crimes involving serious injury or significant property damage.

17. Scientist: The FDA has yet to weigh in on the effects of electronic cigarettes on long-term health. Electronic cigarettes heat up a liquid and produce the vapor inhaled by the user. The liquid consists of vegetable glycerin and propylene glycerol in varying ratios. Artificial flavoring is also added to the liquid. Although the FDA has approved vegetable glycerin, propylene glycerol, and artificial flavors for consumption, little is known about the effects of consuming their vapors. However, electronic cigarettes do not produce tar, which is one of the most dangerous chemicals in tobacco cigarettes.
Which one of the following most accurately expresses the scientist's main point?
    a. The FDA is inefficient and ineffective at protecting public health.
    b. Electronic cigarettes' liquid is probably safer than tobacco.
    c. Smokers should quit tobacco and start using electronic cigarettes.
    d. Tar is the reason why cigarettes are unhealthy.
    e. Although all of the information is not yet available, electronic cigarettes are promising alternatives to tobacco since the former does not produce tar.

18. Sociologist: Poverty is the number one cause of crime. When basic needs, like food and shelter, are not met, people become more willing to engage in criminal activity. The easiest way to reduce crime is to lessen poverty.
Which one of the following statements, if true, best supports the sociologist's argument?
    a. The typical criminal is less wealthy than the average person.
    b. The easiest way to lessen poverty is to redistribute wealth.
    c. Drug addiction and substance use is the second largest cause of crime, and drug users who struggle with addiction are more impoverished than the average person.
    d. Moral societies should guarantee that all their members' basic needs are met.
    e. Studies show that most crimes involve food theft and trespassing.

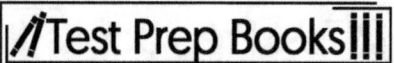

19. West Korea's economy is experiencing high rates of growth for the sixth consecutive quarter. An autocratic despot dominates all aspects of West Korean society, and as a result, West Koreans enjoy less civil liberties and freedom than neighboring countries. Clearly, civil liberties do not impact economic gains.

The following, if true, strengthens the argument, EXCEPT:
   a. Neighboring countries' democratic processes are often deadlocked and unable to respond to immediate economic problems.
   b. The autocratic despot started governing the country six quarters ago.
   c. West Korea found a massive oil reserve under the country shortly before the autocratic despot seized power.
   d. Political protests in neighboring countries often shorten workdays and limit productivity.
   e. The West Korean autocratic despot devotes all of his time to solving economic problems.

20. Sociologist: Marriage is one of the most important societal institutions. The marital relationship provides numerous structural benefits for married couples and their offspring. Studies consistently show that children born out of wedlock are less likely to attend college and more likely to work low-paying jobs. Additionally, married people are more likely to be homeowners and save for retirement. Therefore, if marriage rates decline, _____.

Which one of the following most logically completes the sociologist's argument?
   a. Society will collapse.
   b. Everyone would have less money.
   c. Nobody would own homes.
   d. People would be happier.
   e. College attendance would probably decline.

21. Economist: Countries with lower tax rates tend to have stronger economies. Although higher taxes raise more revenue, highly taxed consumers have less disposable income. An economy can never grow if consumers aren't able to purchase goods and services. Therefore, the government should lower tax rates across the board.

The economist's argument depends on assuming that:
   a. The top five world economies have the lowest tax rates in the world.
   b. Consumers' disposable income is directly related to their ability to purchase goods and services.
   c. Lower tax rates will be much more popular with consumers.
   d. Increasing disposable income is the only way to ensure economic growth.
   e. Economic growth is more important than supporting social welfare programs.

22. The United States' economy continues to grow. Over the last decade, the country's Gross Domestic Product—the monetary value of all finished goods and services produced within a country's borders—has increased by between 2 and 4 percent. The United States' economy is guaranteed to grow between 2 and 4 percent next year.

The flawed reasoning in which of the following arguments most mirrors the flawed reasoning presented in the argument above?

   a. Ted is obsessed with apple pie. He's consumed one whole pie every day for the last decade. Ted will probably eat a whole apple pie tomorrow.
   b. Last year Alexandra finished as the top salesperson at her company. She will undoubtedly be the top salesperson next year.
   c. George always brushes his teeth right before getting into bed. His bedtime routine has remained the same for two decades. It's more probable than not that George brushes his teeth right before getting into bed tomorrow night.
   d. Germany's economy is the strongest it's been since the end of World War II. Over the last decade, the country's Gross Domestic Product—the monetary value of all finished goods and services produced within a country's borders—has increased by between 2 and 4 percent. Germany's economic growth is a result of inclusive democratic processes.
   e. Tito is the top ranked surfer in the world. Las Vegas bookmakers listed him as a clear favorite to win the upcoming invitational tournament. Tito is more likely to win the invitational than any other surfer.

23. Zookeeper: Big cats are undoubtedly among the smartest land mammals. Lions, tigers, and jaguars immediately adjust to their new surroundings. Other animals refuse to eat or drink in captivity, but the big cats relish their timely prepared meals. Big cats never attempt to escape their enclosures.

Which one of the following, if true, most weakens the zookeeper's argument?

   a. Big cats don't attempt to escape because they can't figure out their enclosures' weak spots.
   b. No qualified expert believes that adjusting to captivity is a measure of intelligence.
   c. Bears also do not have any trouble adjusting to captivity.
   d. A recent study comparing the brain scans of large mammals revealed that big cats exhibit the most brain activity when stimulated.
   e. Zoos devote exponentially more resources to big cats relative to other animals.

Data Insights

Multi-Source Reasoning

Prompt 1
Currently, the only health insurance plan offered to a certain company's employees is a zero-deductible plan, and its monthly premium is expensive for the employees. A zero deductible plan means that employees do not have to pay a minimum balance before insurance contributes to health care expenses. Currently, the insurance plan pays 90% of all covered medical costs. However, this plan comes at a high cost to the employees, and there will be more options given in open enrollment this year.

Email Announcement: We are changing our company health insurance plan next year. Instead of the flat monthly fee of $500 for 90% coverage, there will be 4 different options for single employees. Details about family plans will be made available next week. The 4 options for single employees are given in the following excerpts:

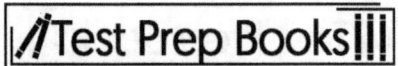

Practice Test #2

Excerpt 1
Single employees will keep the same level of coverage (90% of covered medical costs), and instead of paying $500 monthly for health insurance, they will have $250 taken out of each biweekly paycheck.

Excerpt 2
A new option is a high deductible plan. With this plan, employees will have $50 taken out of each biweekly paycheck. Single employees will have a $5,000 deductible. After $5,000 is spent on medical costs, insurance will cover 90% of covered medical costs.

Excerpt 3
A second new option is a different deductible. With this plan, single employees will have $100 taken out of each paycheck. Employees selecting this option will have a $3,000 deductible. After the deductible is spent on medical costs, insurance will cover 85% of covered medical costs.

Excerpt 4
A final option involves a low deductible option. This plan involves $200 taken out of each paycheck, and single employees selecting this option will have a $1,000 deductible. After this amount is spent on medical costs, insurance will cover 80% of covered medical costs.

1. Based on the information provided, answer the following questions.

Yes	No	
○	○	The employees who select the same plan (with no deductible) will be paying the same yearly amount.
○	○	The high deductible plan will be selected the most often because it is the least expensive.
○	○	The low deductible plan will cost each single employee $5,200 a year.

2. Based on the information provided, answer the following questions.

Yes	No	
○	○	An employee who estimates that she will have $10,000 in total covered medical costs next year should choose the high deductible plan.
○	○	An employee who anticipates no medical bills should choose the high deductible plan.
○	○	An employee who estimates that he will have $100,000 in total covered medical costs next year should choose the high deductible plan.

Prompt 2:
Announcement: We are excited to announce that we are overhauling our tuition costs for the 2019–2020 school year. Instead of paying a flat rate per credit hour, student who take more credit hours will have discounts applied. Currently, in-state students pay $650 per credit hour and out-of-state students pay $1,050 per credit hour. These costs will change in the following manner:

Students taking between 1 and 6 credit hours will pay the same amount per credit hour, with a 1% increase next year.

Students taking between 7 and 10 credit hours will pay the same 1% increase per credit hour, but they will receive a 10% discount on their tuition.

Students taking between 11 and 15 credit hours will also see a 1% increase per credit hour, but will receive a 15% discount on tuition.

Students taking between 16 and 18 credit hours will pay a 1% increase per credit hour, and they will receive a 20% discount on total tuition.

Students taking more than 18 credit hours receive the 20% discount for the first 18 credit hours of tuition; every credit hour taken after 18 is subject to the cost of taking a single credit hour.

We are also reworking the enrollment process. Students who plan to take more than 15 credit hours will select classes on the first Monday in April. Students who plan to take between 11 and 15 credit hours will select classes on the second Monday in April. Finally, students who plan to take fewer than 11 credit hours will select classes on the third Monday in April.

We hope that these changes encourage students to take more credit hours each semester in order to graduate sooner.

3. Calculate the cost of taking 12 credit hours as an out-of-state resident in the 2019–2020 school year. Round to the nearest dollar.
   a. $10,817
   b. $12,726
   c. $12,600
   d. $10,710
   e. $1,909

4. Based on the information provided, answer the following questions.

Yes	No	
○	○	A student registering for 4 credit hours next year will enroll after a student registering for 9 credit hours.
○	○	A student who takes the same number of credit hours as in the previous year will pay a 1% increase in tuition next year.
○	○	An in-state student taking 19 credit hours next year will pay $10,110.10.

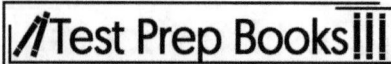

Practice Test #2

Graphic Interpretation

5. The table below shows the number of employees at XYZ Cable Company and their corresponding years of service at the company. What percent of total employees have worked at XYZ Cable Company for between 5 and 10 years? Round your answer to the nearest tenth of a percent.

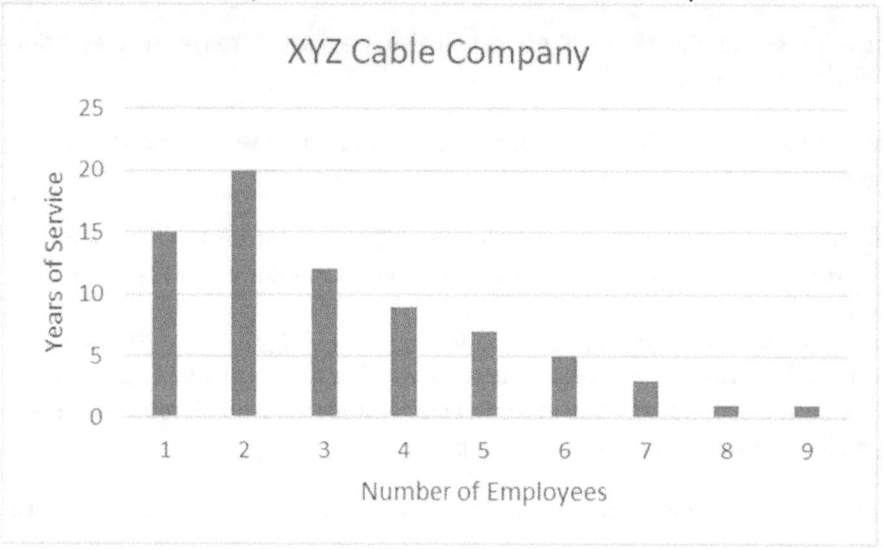

a. 11.1%
b. 33.3%
c. 84.4%
d. 8.9%

6. The graph shows the position of a car over a 10-second time interval. Which of the following is the correct interpretation of the graph for the interval 1 to 3 seconds?

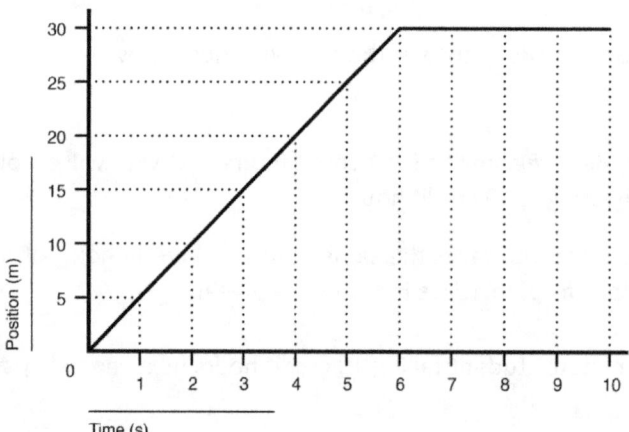

a. The car remains in the same position.
b. The car is traveling at a speed of 5 m/s.
c. The car is traveling up a hill.
d. The car is traveling at 5 mph.
e. The car is traveling at a speed of 10 m/s.

7. The chart below shows the percentage (rounded to the nearest tenth of a percent) of seniors from Heights High School and their plans for after high school. The number of seniors planning to attend a four-year college or university is 267. How many total seniors are planning to go into the military? Round your answer to the nearest integer.

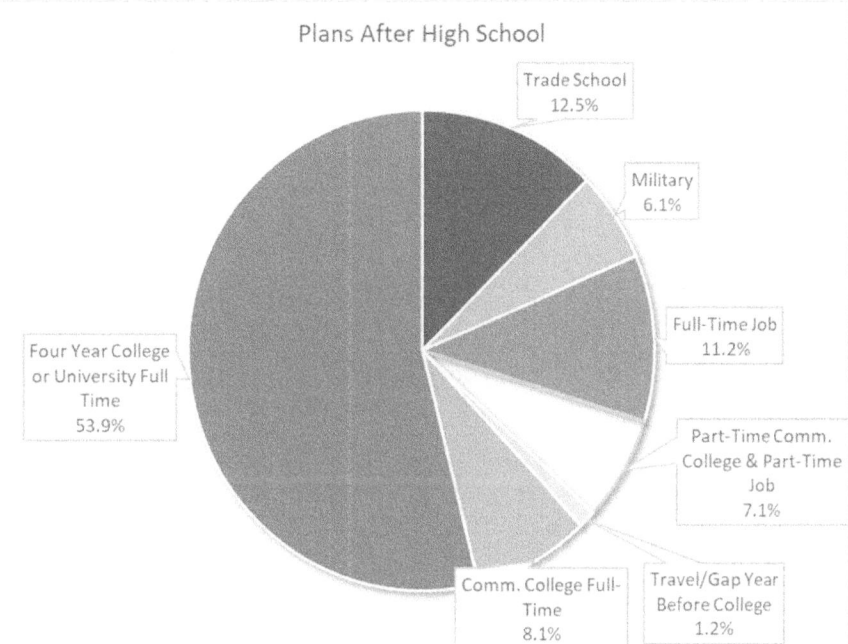

a. 495
b. 29
c. 46
d. 30

8. The graph below is a scatter plot with 30 points that correspond to the number of miles driven in a given time period for a truck driver this year. The time is given in hours. The dashed line refers to the regression line. Based on the regression line, if the truck driver drives for 7 hours, approximately how far will he go?

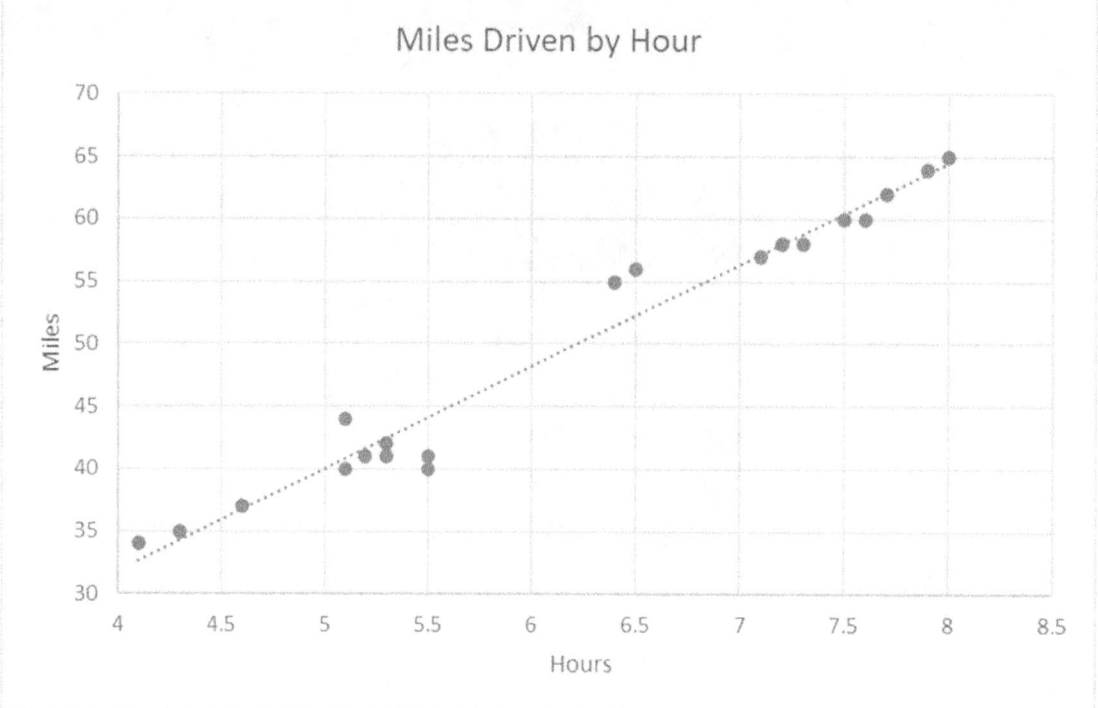

a. 55 miles
b. 57 miles
c. 60 miles
d. 50 miles

Two-Part Analysis

9. The quotient $\frac{x}{y}$ is a multiple of 9.

In the table below, choose the value of x and the value of y that are consistent with this statement. Make only one selection for x and one selection for y.

x	y	
○	○	56
○	○	135
○	○	1,176
○	○	15

10. At the state university, there are 1,350 business majors. There are 3 times as many marketing majors as accounting majors, and there are 50 students who are double majors in both accounting and marketing. The state university offers no other business degrees. In the table below, choose the number of accounting majors and the number of marketing majors consistent with this information. Make only one selection for each major.

Accounting	Marketing	
○	○	350
○	○	250
○	○	1,050
○	○	1,150

Table Analysis

11. U.S. Internet Sales in 2017 of the ABC Cable Company.

		Package Selection		
		Basic Package	Deluxe Package	Extra Deluxe Package
Region	Northeast	40.4	55.1	20.1
	Midwest	45.2	60.3	15.8
	South	34.1	41.2	23.1
	West	16.1	22.3	13.2

Note: All numbers above are in thousands.

TRUE	FALSE	
○	○	The average number of basic packages sold was 135,800.
○	○	The percentage of packages sold that were not basic was approximately 35%.
○	○	The region with the largest number of internet sales for the ABC Cable Company was the Midwest.

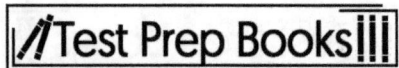

12.

Student	Credit Hours Completed	Major	ACT Score
Joe	18	Physical Therapy	31
Michael	16	Pre-Med	30
Kayla	14	Chemistry	28
Kendra	13	Mathematics	24
Mitchell	17	English	27
Alice	12	Nursing	31
Edward	17	Biology	32
Trista	18	Nursing	29
Kyle	19	Pre-Med	27
Stella	12	Physical Therapy	28
Rita	14	Engineering	31
Robert	14	Interior Design	30
Barry	15	Engineering	25

TRUE	FALSE	
○	○	The average number of credits completed was 16.
○	○	The probability that a student is an engineering major is higher than the probability that a student is a physical therapy major.
○	○	The data set corresponding to the ACT scores is bimodal.

13.

Year	Population of State X	Population of State Y	Population of State Z
2001	300.1	250.3	185.2
2002	301.2	251.4	185.1
2003	299.9	250.9	184.7
2004	298.8	251.1	184.9
2005	299.5	251	184.2
2006	300.2	251.7	183.9
2007	300.3	252	183.8
2008	301.1	252.3	184.5
2009	302.1	252.5	184.3
2010	301.3	252.7	185

Note: Populations shown in thousands.

TRUE	FALSE	
○	○	The largest percent change for the population in State X occurred from 2002 to 2003.
○	○	The largest percent decrease for the population in State Y occurred from 2001 to 2002.
○	○	The population in State Z increased by the same percentage from 2007 to 2008 as it decreased from 2004 to 2005.

Data Sufficiency

Decide whether the data given in the statements are sufficient to answer the question.

14. Katie is delivering 4 packages today. In how many ways can she select the packages that she delivers?

  1) She never delivers more than 5 packages at once.

  2) Her employer has 10 packages available to deliver.

  a. Statement (1) ALONE is sufficient, but statement (2) ALONE is NOT sufficient.
  b. Statement (2) ALONE is sufficient, but statement (1) ALONE is NOT sufficient.
  c. BOTH statements TOGETHER are sufficient, but NEITHER statement ALONE is sufficient.
  d. EACH statement ALONE is sufficient.
  e. Statements (1) and (2) TOGETHER are NOT sufficient.

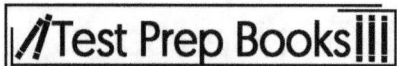

15. Katie and Serena are writing a story for a newspaper. Katie can write at a speed 2 times faster than Serena can. How long will it take them to finish the story while working together?

   1) Working individually, Katie could finish the story in 4 hours.

   2) Serena can write 1,500 words per hour.

   a. Statement (1) ALONE is sufficient, but statement (2) ALONE is NOT sufficient.
   b. Statement (2) ALONE is sufficient, but statement (1) ALONE is NOT sufficient.
   c. BOTH statements TOGETHER are sufficient, but NEITHER statement ALONE is sufficient.
   d. EACH statement ALONE is sufficient.
   e. Statements (1) and (2) TOGETHER are NOT sufficient.

16. Is $9 - \frac{x}{9}$ an integer?

   1) x is a multiple of 6.

   2) The process of the division of x by 9 results in a zero remainder.

   a. Statement (1) ALONE is sufficient, but statement (2) ALONE is NOT sufficient.
   b. Statement (2) ALONE is sufficient, but statement (1) ALONE is NOT sufficient.
   c. BOTH statements TOGETHER are sufficient, but NEITHER statement ALONE is sufficient.
   d. EACH statement ALONE is sufficient.
   e. Statements (1) and (2) TOGETHER are NOT sufficient.

17. To stock your grocery store, you purchase boxes of oatmeal from your supplier for $2 each and sell them to customers. How much do you individually sell them for?

   1) Your profit from each sale is 25%.

   2) The amount that you pay for the oatmeal is 80% of what you sell it for.

   a. Statement (1) ALONE is sufficient, but statement (2) ALONE is NOT sufficient.
   b. Statement (2) ALONE is sufficient, but statement (1) ALONE is NOT sufficient.
   c. BOTH statements TOGETHER are sufficient, but NEITHER statement ALONE is sufficient.
   d. EACH statement ALONE is sufficient.
   e. Statements (1) and (2) TOGETHER are NOT sufficient.

18. A set consists of the total snowfall for 7 days. Is the median of the set less than the mode?

   1) The mean and median of the set are equal to 3.

   2) The mode appears twice in the set.

   a. Statement (1) ALONE is sufficient, but statement (2) ALONE is NOT sufficient.
   b. Statement (2) ALONE is sufficient, but statement (1) ALONE is NOT sufficient.
   c. BOTH statements TOGETHER are sufficient, but NEITHER statement ALONE is sufficient.
   d. EACH statement ALONE is sufficient.
   e. Statements (1) and (2) TOGETHER are NOT sufficient.

19. The dimensions of a rectangular box are 7 centimeters by 11 centimeters by 12 centimeters. If a cylinder is placed inside the box so that either circular end touches the top and bottom of the box, what is the volume of the circular cylinder?

   1) The surface area of the cylinder is 128π square centimeters.

   2) The base of a box has an area of 77 square centimeters.

   a. Statement (1) ALONE is sufficient, but statement (2) ALONE is NOT sufficient.
   b. Statement (2) ALONE is sufficient, but statement (1) ALONE is NOT sufficient.
   c. BOTH statements TOGETHER are sufficient, but NEITHER statement ALONE is sufficient.
   d. EACH statement ALONE is sufficient.
   e. Statements (1) and (2) TOGETHER are NOT sufficient.

20. A bag contains only red, green, and blue marbles. In total, there are 39 marbles in the bag. What is the probability of pulling a red marble from the bag?

   1) There are 14 blue marbles.

   2) The probability of selecting a green marble is equal to the probability of selecting a blue marble.

   a. Statement (1) ALONE is sufficient, but statement (2) ALONE is NOT sufficient.
   b. Statement (2) ALONE is sufficient, but statement (1) ALONE is NOT sufficient.
   c. BOTH statements TOGETHER are sufficient, but NEITHER statement ALONE is sufficient.
   d. EACH statement ALONE is sufficient.
   e. Statements (1) and (2) TOGETHER are NOT sufficient.

Answer Explanations #2

Quantitative Reasoning

Problem Solving

1. B: The first step is to make all exponents positive by moving the terms with negative exponents to the opposite side of the fraction. This expression becomes:

$$\frac{4b^3 b^2}{a^1 a^4} \times \frac{3a}{b}$$

Then the rules for exponents can be used to simplify. Multiplying the same bases means the exponents can be added. Dividing the same bases means the exponents are subtracted. Thus, after multiplying the exponents in the first fraction, the expression becomes:

$$\frac{4b^5}{a^5} \times \frac{3a}{b}$$

Therefore, we can first multiply to get:

$$\frac{12ab^5}{a^5 b}$$

Then, simplifying yields:

$$12\frac{b^4}{a^4}$$

2. E: The product of two irrational numbers can be rational or irrational. Sometimes the irrational parts of the two numbers cancel each other out, leaving a rational number. For example, $\sqrt{2} \times \sqrt{2} = 2$ because the roots cancel each other out. Technically, the product of two irrational numbers is a complex number, because real numbers are a type of complex number. However, Choice D is incorrect because the product of two irrational numbers is not an imaginary number.

3. C: The terms "whole numbers" and "natural numbers" include all the ordinary counting numbers (1, 2, 3, 4, 5, ...), and sometimes zero depending on the definition used, but no negative numbers. The term "integers" includes all those numbers, their negatives, and zero. So –4 is not a whole number or a natural number, but it is an integer. It is also rational because it can be written as a ratio of two integers ($-\frac{4}{1}$); all integers are rational. It is a real number because it does not have an imaginary component (symbolized by the letter i); all integers are real numbers.

4. D: If $n = 2^2, n = 4$, and $m = 4^2 = 16$. This means that $m^n = 16^4$. But all the answer choices are written as powers of 2, so we can calculate:

$$16^4 = (2^4)^4 = 2^{4 \times 4} = 2^{16}$$

Answer Explanations #2

5. E: The first step in solving this equation is to collect like terms on the left side of the equation. This yields the new equation $-4 + 8x = 8 - 10x$. The next step is to move the x-terms to one side by adding $10x$ to both sides, making the equation $-4 + 18x = 8$. Then the -4 can be moved to the right side of the equation to form $18x = 12$. Dividing both sides of the equation by 18 gives a value of 0.67, or $\frac{2}{3}$.

6. B: There are two zeros for the function: $x = 0, -2$. The zeros can be found several ways, but this particular equation can be factored into:

$$f(x) = x(x^2 + 4x + 4) = x(x+2)(x+2)$$

By setting each factor equal to zero and solving for x, there are two solutions. On a graph, these zeros can be seen where the line crosses the x-axis.

7. D: This problem involves a composition function, where one function is plugged into the other function. In this case, the $f(x)$ function is plugged into the $g(x)$ function for each x value. Since $f(x) = 2$, the composition equation becomes:

$$g(f(x)) = g(2) = (2)^3 - 3(2)^2 - 2(2) + 6$$

Simplifying the equation gives the answer:

$$g(f(x)) = 8 - 3(4) - 2(2) + 6$$

$$8 - 12 - 4 + 6 = -2$$

8. D: This system of equations involves one quadratic equation and one linear equation. One way to solve this is through substitution.

Solving for y in the second equation yields:

$$y = x + 2$$

Plugging this equation in for the y of the quadratic equation yields:

$$x^2 - 2x + x + 2 = 8$$

Simplify the equation:

$$x^2 - x + 2 = 8$$

Set this equal to zero and factor:

$$x^2 - x - 6 = 0 = (x-3)(x+2)$$

Solving these two factors for x gives the zeros:

$$x = 3, -2$$

To find the y-value for the point, plug in each number to either original equation. Solving each one for y yields the points $(3,5)$ and $(-2,0)$.

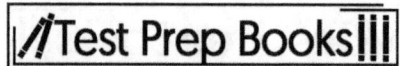

Answer Explanations #2

9. D: The expression is simplified by collecting like terms. Terms with the same variable and exponent are like terms, and their coefficients can be added.

10. A: Finding the product means distributing one polynomial onto the other. Each term in the first polynomial must be multiplied by each term in the second polynomial. Then, like terms can be collected. Multiplying the factors yields the expression:

$$20x^3 + 4x^2 + 24x - 40x^2 - 8x - 48$$

Collecting like terms means adding the x^2 terms and adding the x terms. Then, simplify:

$$20x^3 - 36x^2 + 16x - 48$$

11. E: Finding the zeros for a function by factoring is done by setting the equation equal to zero, then completely factoring. Since there is a common x for each term in the provided equation, that should be factored out first. Then the quadratic that is left can be factored into two binomials, which are $(x + 1)(x - 4)$. Setting each factor equal to zero and solving for x yields three zeros.

12. D: Dividing rational expressions follows the same rule as dividing fractions. The division is changed to multiplication by the reciprocal of the second fraction. This turns the expression into:

$$\frac{5x^3}{3x^2y} \times \frac{3y^9}{25}$$

This can be simplified by finding common factors in the numerators and denominators of the two fractions.

$$\frac{x^3}{x^2y} \times \frac{y^9}{5}$$

Multiplying across creates:

$$\frac{x^3 y^9}{5x^2 y}$$

Simplifying leads to the final expression of:

$$\frac{xy^8}{5}$$

13. B: We can try to solve the equation by factoring the numerator into $(x + 6)(x - 5)$. Since the factor $(x - 5)$ is in the numerator and the denominator, it cancels out. This leaves the equation:

$$x + 6 = 11$$

Solving the equation gives the answer $x = 5$. When this value is plugged into the equation, it yields a zero in the denominator of the fraction. Since this is undefined, there is no solution.

14. D: This problem can be solved by using unit conversion. The initial units are miles per minute. The final units need to be feet per second. Converting miles to feet uses the equivalence statement 1 mi =

112

5,280 ft. Converting minutes to seconds uses the equivalence statement 1 min = 60 s. Setting up the ratios to convert the units is shown in the following equation:

$$\frac{72 \text{ mi}}{90 \text{ min}} \times \frac{1 \text{ min}}{60 \text{ s}} \times \frac{5{,}280 \text{ ft}}{1 \text{ mi}} = 70.4 \frac{\text{ft}}{\text{s}}$$

The initial units cancel out, and the new units are left.

15. B: The formula can be manipulated by dividing both the length, l, and the width, w, on both sides. The length and width will cancel on the right, leaving height, h, by itself.

16. B: The domain is all possible input values, or x-values. For this equation, the domain is every number greater than or equal to zero. There are no negative numbers in the domain because taking the square root of a negative number results in an imaginary number.

17. E: This problem can be solved by setting up a proportion involving the given information and the unknown value. The proportion is:

$$\frac{21 \text{ pages}}{4 \text{ nights}} = \frac{140 \text{ pages}}{x \text{ nights}}$$

We can cross-multiply to get $21x = 4 \times 140$. Solving this, we find $x \approx 26.67$. Since this is not an integer, we round up to 27 nights because 26 nights would not give Sarah enough time to finish.

18. D: The slope from this equation is 50, and it is interpreted as the cost per gigabyte used. Since the g-value represents the number of gigabytes and the equation is set equal to the cost in dollars, the slope relates these two values. For every gigabyte used on the phone, the bill goes up 50 dollars.

19. A: The ratio of fruit to vegetables is 5 to 3, which means that 3 out of every 8 produce items are vegetables. $\frac{3}{8} = 0.375$, and $0.375 \times 120 = 45$. Therefore, 45 of the total 120 produce items are vegetables and $120 - 45 = 75$ are fruit.

20. B: The given rate is equal to $\frac{18}{4} = \frac{9}{2}$ miles per hour. Choice A is equal to $\frac{4}{36} = \frac{1}{9}$, so this is not a correct option. Choice B is equal to $\frac{36}{8} = \frac{9}{2}$, so this is a correct option. Choice C is incorrect because it inaccurately simplifies $\frac{36}{8}$ to $\frac{9}{4}$, dividing the denominator by 2 instead of 4. Choice D simplifies to $\frac{180}{20} = 9$, and this is not equal to the given rate. Finally, Choice E is equal to $\frac{4}{9}$, which is an incorrect option. The only equivalent proportion is Choice B.

21. E: The answer is 64. The first step is to find the value of m. Recall that roots of numbers are the same as fractional exponents:

$$\sqrt[3]{m} = m^{\frac{1}{3}} = 2$$

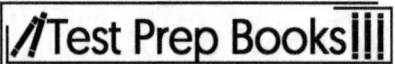

Answer Explanations #2

Both sides of the equation can be raised to the power of 3 to solve for m. Using the power rule, an exponent on an exponent results in multiplying the exponents, canceling out the cube root:

$$\left(m^{\frac{1}{3}}\right)^3 = m^{\frac{1}{3} \times 3} = m = 2^3$$

$$m = 8$$

Using the value of m, solve the second equation for n:

$$m = 8 = \sqrt{n}$$

$$n = 8^2$$

$$n = 64$$

Therefore, the correct answer is Choice E, 64.

Verbal Reasoning

Reading Comprehension

1. D: The passage references statements made by the World Bank in 1995 at the end of the first paragraph and in the middle of the second. The first reference says that state-owned enterprises "remain an important obstacle to better economic performance," and the second reference says the "World Bank recommended that SOEs be corporatized under commercial law and issued guidance." Thus, Choice A is incorrect and Choice D is correct. Although the World Bank is probably discussing developing countries, they are not mentioned in the statements quoted in the passage, so Choice B is incorrect. Choice C is not stated by the passage and never mentioned in connection with statements issued by the World Bank. While the passage draws conclusions similar to what's described in Choice E, they are not included in the World Bank's statements.

2. B: The passage repeatedly mentions disputes over privatization, including inconclusive studies, scholars refuting the World Bank's statements about state-owned enterprises, and differences between free market advocates who want to "unleash" the private sector and the World Bank's more gradual approach. Thus, Choice B is the correct answer. Choice A is incorrect because "always" is too strong. The studies are inconclusive and have yielded conflicting results. Choice C is incorrect for similar reasons. Although the studies in this passage are criticized, it's too much to say economic studies in general are always subject to such criticism. The World Bank recommends that state-owned enterprises be privatized in accordance with commercial law, but that doesn't necessarily mean those enterprises violate commercial law, so Choice D is incorrect. Nowhere in the passage does it say the World Bank holds the power to intervene in economies; its statements are referred to as recommendations. Thus, Choice E is incorrect.

3. E: World Bank includes competition and corporate governance free of political interference in its five preconditions for successful privatization, making Choice E the correct answer. The passage states that state-owned enterprises have a "pervasive presence" in the global economy, making Choice D incorrect. The empirical research is inconclusive but, if anything, it leans toward the opposite of what's described

Answer Explanations #2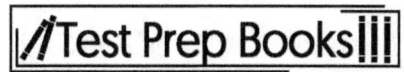

in Choice A. Influences on the World Bank's policies and popular support for privatization are never mentioned in the passage; therefore, Choices B and C are incorrect.

4. C: The author's conclusion is that "SOEs are an entity to be considered and managed in the pursuit of stability." The passage does not present a conclusion on whether privatization is an effective strategy. Thus, Choice C is the correct answer. Choice A is not supported by the passage. Choices B and D are likely among the author's assumptions, but they are not conclusions. Choice E reflects the World Bank's position, but is not necessarily what the author believes.

5. C: The author mentions in the third paragraph how apologia focuses on the short term and reconciliation has long-term goals. Thus, Choice C is correct. Choice D is incorrect because reconciliation seeks to open channels of communication, not close them. The first clause in Choice A describes reconciliation rather than apologia, so it's incorrect. Choice B is incorrect because it's never stated or implied that apologia is always delivered in writing. The author doesn't claim that apologia requires actually receiving forgiveness to be effective, and reconciliation involves more than just delivering visual responses, so Choice E is incorrect.

6. E: The author states that national leaders use apologia and reconciliation to restore their image, so it can be inferred that a positive national image is an important part of governance. Thus, Choice E is the correct answer. The author favors reconciliation, but it's unlikely she would agree that national leaders should never apologize. Thus, Choice A is incorrect. Similarly, the author implies that apologia is self-serving but, as described by the author, reconciliation also seems to be self-serving. In any event, the author thinks reconciliation is generally more effective because of its long-term effect, not because it's less self-serving. Thus, Choice B is incorrect. Choices C and D are never mentioned or alluded to in the passage, so they cannot be properly inferred.

7. B: Reconciliation's use of symbolic visual images and impact on the long-term relationship between the aggrieved and the transgressor is described in the third paragraph. Thus, Choice B is the correct answer. Choice A is incorrect because reconciliation involves long term, not short term, repair. The other answer choices describe features of apologia, not reconciliation, so Choices C, D, and E are all incorrect.

8. E: The author states in the fourth paragraph that offending images don't always require a visual response, but when they do, reconciliation is the better choice due to its long-term goals. Thus, Choice E is the correct answer. Censorship and anti-propaganda campaigns are never mentioned in the passage, so Choices A and B are incorrect. Choices C and D are incorrect because they are directly contradicted in the fourth paragraph.

9. C: The first sentence of the second paragraph states, "While spending more than other countries per capita on health care services, the United States spends less on average than do other nations on social services impacting social and behavioral determinants of health." Thus, Choice A is incorrect and C is correct. Choice B is incorrect because it reverses the United States' ratio. The author argues that America's lower life expectancy is due to lower spending on social services, not insufficient funding for health care, so Choice D is incorrect. Choice E is incorrect because the United States does fund interdisciplinary programs that include behavioral and social science, like the Clinical and Translational Science Awards.

10. B: The Clinical and Translational Science Awards are mentioned in the third paragraph, and the author states that its interdisciplinary programs "aim to advance the translation of research findings

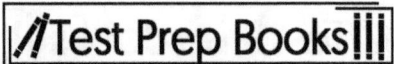

Answer Explanations #2

from 'bench' to 'bedside' to 'community.'" Thus, Choice B is the correct answer. The Clinical and Translational Science Awards would likely support expanding social services, but advocating for that position isn't their purpose, so Choice A is incorrect. Similarly, the Clinical and Translational Science Awards likely conduct research on behavioral risks, but that's only part of the larger goal. So, Choice C is incorrect. Choice D is incorrect because employing social and behavioral scientists is not the Clinical and Translational Science Awards' primary purpose. It's unclear whether the Clinical and Translational Science Awards would even be involved in policy questions like calculating the optimal ratio for government spending, so Choice E isn't the primary purpose.

11. C: The author repeatedly mentions how the United States neglects social services. According to the author, this is why the United States performs poorly on key health indicators despite spending more per capita on health care than any other country. In addition, the author argues that the Clinical and Translational Science Awards should hire more social and behavioral scientists. Thus, Choice C is the correct answer. Choices A and D are premises that support the conclusion, not the main thesis, so they are both incorrect. Choice B is incorrect because it's only providing background information about the Clinical and Translational Science Awards. The author never asserts that life expectancy is the most important health care indicator, and, even if that were true, it wouldn't be the main thesis. Thus, Choice E is incorrect.

12. A: The purpose is to inform the reader about what assault is and how it is committed. Choice B is incorrect because the passage does not state that assault is a lesser form of lethal force, only that an assault can use lethal force, or alternatively, lethal force can be utilized to counter a dangerous assault. Choices C and D are incorrect because the passage is informative and does not have a set agenda. Finally, Choice E is incorrect because although the author uses an example in order to explain assault, it is not indicated that this is the author's personal account.

13. B: As discussed in the second passage, there are several forms of assault, like assault with a deadly weapon, verbal assault, or threatening posture or language. Choice A is incorrect because lethal force and assault are separate, as indicated by the passages. Choice C is incorrect because anyone is capable of assault; the author does not state that one group of people cannot commit assault. Choice D is incorrect because assault is never justified. Self-defense resulting in lethal force can be justified. Choice E is incorrect because the author does not mention what the charges are on assaults; therefore, we cannot assume that they are more or less severe than unnecessary use of force charges.

14. A: Both passages open by defining a legal concept and then describing situations in order to further explain the concept. Choice D is incorrect because while the passages utilize examples to help explain the concepts discussed, the author doesn't indicate that they are specific court cases. It's also clear that the passages don't open with examples but instead begin by defining the terms addressed in each passage. This eliminates Choice B and ultimately reveals Choice A to be the correct answer. Choice A accurately outlines the way both passages are structured. Because the passages follow a nearly identical structure, the rest of the choices can be ruled out.

Critical Reasoning

15. C: Choice A is not present in the teacher's argument. There is no discussion of a common rule, so this cannot be the answer. Eliminate this choice.

Choice *B* is inaccurate. The teacher justifies his argument by pointing to the two highest achieving students in his class. It's not a perfect argument, but it's untrue to say that the argument is totally unjustified.

Choice *C* looks much more promising than the other options. The teacher's conclusion is that it's *always* the case that students can overcome parental indifference. He supports this notion by pointing to the two best students in a class of twenty people. The conclusion is too broad when considering the evidence. This is probably the answer, but look at the other choices to make sure.

Choice *D* does not correspond with anything in the teacher's argument. Although the teacher doesn't present any counter arguments, the existence of a competing theory is unclear. Eliminate this choice.

Choice *E* is clearly incorrect. The argument does not show any bias. Eliminate this choice.

Therefore, Choice *C* is the correct answer.

16. C: Choice *A* restates a premise and does not resolve the paradox. Whether Trent's SWAT team is the best police unit does not answer why unsolved crimes are increasing every year despite historic rates of crime solving. Eliminate this choice.

Choice *B* also does not resolve the paradox. It attempts to dismiss the increase in unsolved crimes by characterizing those crimes as petty drug offenses. Even if true, this does not resolve the paradox.

Choice *C* is a strong answer choice. If the raw number of crimes increases every year, then it makes sense that crimes are increasing despite the historic rates of crime solving. This explains the paradox. In questions involving percentages, always pay special attention to answer choices that involve raw numbers.

Choice *D* is irrelevant. The competence of the police department does not explain the paradox. Additionally, the police department is apparently not incompetent since it's solving a higher percentage of crimes than ever before in its history. Eliminate this choice.

Choice *E* is similar to Choice *B*. It attempts to dismiss the increasing number of unsolved crimes by claiming that the police are solving the most important crimes. This does not explain the paradox.

Therefore, Choice *C* is the correct answer.

17. E: Choice *A* is unrelated to the argument's main point. This choice is misleading with extraneous information because the FDA is often criticized for this very reason. However, the argument does not address this point. There's no way it's the main point. Eliminate this choice.

Choice *B* is a very strong answer. The argument is definitely trending in this direction, especially since the argument points out the lack of tar in electronic cigarettes. Choice *B*'s use of *probably* fits with the argument's tone. Leave this option for now.

Choice *C* goes too far. The scientist's argument is more informational than directional. Choice *C* fails to match this tone. Eliminate this choice.

Choice *D* accurately restates one of the argument's premises, but it is not the main point. Eliminate this choice.

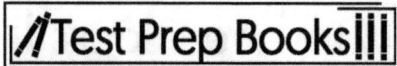

Answer Explanations #2

Choice E is an excellent balance of information and speculation, like the argument. The answer choice's first phrase identifies the concerns highlighted by the scientist, and the second phrase expresses why the scientist believes that electronic cigarettes are a promising alternative. Choice B is extremely similar, but Choice E better expresses the argument's main point.

Therefore, Choice E is the correct answer.

18. E: Choice A supports the argument. The argument concludes that poverty is the number one cause of crime. It would make sense that criminals are less wealthy than the average person. Keep this choice for now.

Choice B is irrelevant for the purposes of this argument. Even if redistributing wealth is indeed the best way to lessen poverty, it does not support the connection between poverty and crime. Eliminate this choice.

Choice C is tangentially related to the argument. If substance abuse is the second largest cause of crime and those abusers are poor, then it makes sense that criminals are poor. However, this answer choice is worse than Choice A, which explicitly states the same thing. Eliminate this choice.

Choice D is irrelevant. The argument makes no mention of morality or how moral societies would treat the poor. Eliminate this choice.

Choice E is a very strong answer. If the majority of crimes involve food theft and trespassing, then it supports the notion that people commit crimes to meet their basic needs. Choice E strengthens the conclusion that if these people's basic needs were met then the majority of crime would not be committed. This offers more support than Choice A.

Therefore, Choice E is the correct answer.

19. C: Choice A definitely strengthens the argument by highlighting a benefit of an autocratic government. Eliminate this choice.

Choice B seems to strengthen the argument. This answer choice connects the start of the autocratic despot's reign with the start of economic growth. Eliminate this choice.

Choice C appears to weaken the argument. This answer choice provides an alternate explanation for the economic growth. According to Choice C, West Korea experienced economic growth as a result of the oil reserve. This hurts the argument's contention that West Korea's economy benefits from limiting civil liberties. This is a very strong answer choice.

Choice D clearly strengthens the argument. If political protest harms economic growth, then there's additional support for West Korea's curtailment of civil liberties. Eliminate this choice.

Choice E also strengthens the argument. The despot is able to devote all of his time to solving economic problems since there are no civil liberties. Eliminate this choice.

Therefore, Choice C is the correct answer.

20. E: Choice A is too extreme. The sociologist definitely believes that the abolition of marriage would harm society, but collapse goes too far. Eliminate this choice.

Answer Explanations #2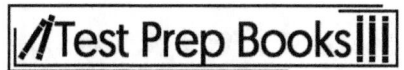

Choice B is tricky since the previous sentence references how children born out of wedlock are more likely to work at lower paying jobs. However, this answer choice also goes too far. According to the argument, unmarried people are less likely to be homeowners or save for retirement. But if marriage rates decline, it is not necessarily true that everyone would have less money. Eliminate this choice.

Choice C is tricky but also incorrect. Unmarried people are less likely to own homes. If marriage rates decline, fewer people would be homeowners. This is not the same as arguing that nobody would own homes. Eliminate this choice.

Choice D is irrelevant to the argument. The argument makes no reference to happiness. There is no way that such new information would logically complete the passage. Eliminate this choice.

Choice E looks much more promising than the other choices. If unmarried people are less likely to attend college and marriage rates decline, then it is reasonable to say that college attendance would probably decrease. Choice E also matches the argument's tone through the use of *probably*, unlike many of the other answer choices.

Therefore, Choice E is the correct answer.

21. B: Choice A is not a necessary assumption. This answer choice provides additional support to the argument, but it is not dependent on this fact. The test developers hope the test takers will mistake this for a strengthening question. Don't be fooled. Eliminate this choice.

Choice B looks very promising. Negate this answer choice to see if the argument falls apart: *Consumers' disposable income is NOT directly related to their ability to purchase goods and services.* This hurts the argument. If disposable income is unrelated to purchasing goods and services, then tax rates don't matter. Definitely keep this answer.

Choice C is irrelevant to the argument. The argument does not depend on consumers' preferences. Eliminate this choice.

Choice D is a strong answer choice. Negate this answer choice to see if the argument falls apart: *Increasing disposable income is NOT the only way to ensure economic growth.* The argument is definitely worse off, but it is not destroyed. Therefore, this is not a necessary assumption. Eliminate this choice.

Choice E is irrelevant to the argument. The argument discusses how tax rates impact economic growth. It does not mention social welfare programs. Always be careful of new information, like the role social welfare programs play in this choice. Eliminate this choice.

Therefore, Choice B is the correct answer.

22. B: Choice A is similar to the argument in that it makes a prediction based on past events; however, Choice A's argument is much more reasonable than the argument. If Ted has eaten an apple pie every day for the last decade, then it's reasonable to assume that he will do so again tomorrow. Eliminate this choice.

Choice B is a very strong answer choice. Like the argument, it takes past events and speculates that conditions will not change. Just as any number of factors could alter the United States' economic growth, it is similarly unreasonable to say that Alexandra will be the top salesperson based on one year's

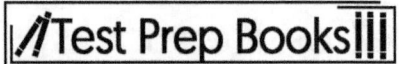

data. This answer choice also uses extremely strong language in its speculation (*guaranteed* and *undoubtedly*). Definitely keep this answer choice as an option.

Choice C is similar to the argument, but its conclusion is much more reasonable. If George has brushed his teeth right before bed for twenty years, then it is not unreasonable to speculate that he will do the same tonight. This is not the same as predicting that past economic conditions will continue into the future. George has much more control over brushing his teeth than the United States has over its economy. Eliminate this choice.

Choice D mirrors the language as the argument, but it draws a very different conclusion. In contrast to the argument, Choice D's conclusion gives a reason why Germany's economy is on the rise. It does not make a guarantee of future growth. This is not the same as the argument. Eliminate this choice.

Choice E does not rely on flawed reasoning, so it must be incorrect. If Tito is the top ranked surfer in the world and listed as a clear favorite, then it's true that he's the most likely to win the tournament. Eliminate this choice.

Therefore, Choice B is the correct answer.

23. B: Choice A weakens one of the argument's premises. If big cats don't try to escape because they can't figure out their enclosures, then never attempting to escape is not a sign of intelligence. This definitely weakens the argument by negating one of its premises. Keep it for now.

Choice B looks extremely promising. This answer choice tells us that experts disagree that adjusting to captivity is a measure of intelligence. If big cats' adjustment to captivity does not correspond to intelligence, then the zookeeper's entire argument is flawed. This destroys the argument.

Choice C weakens the argument, but it's less powerful than Choice B. If bears share similarities with big cats, then there might be some doubt as to which animal is the smartest land mammal. This weakens the argument, but not as much as Choice B, which completely disrupts the argument's logic. Eliminate this choice.

Choice D actually strengthens the zookeeper's argument. The brain scans support the zookeeper's conclusion that big cats are the smartest land mammals. Eliminate this choice.

Choice E is a strong answer choice. If the zoo is devoting significantly more resources to caring for big cats, then the difference in resources could be the reason for their adaptability. However, Choice B spoils the argument's entire logical thrust. Eliminate Choice E.

Therefore, Choice B is the correct answer.

Data Insights

Multi-Source Reasoning

1. NO: The employees in the previous year pay $500 monthly, which totals $6,000 per year. Next year, the employees will pay $250 biweekly, which totals $6,500.

NO: The other plans might make more sense for some employees who anticipate having high medical bills.

Answer Explanations #2

YES: The low deductible plan costs $200 biweekly, which totals $5,200 per year.

2. NO: The high deductible plan will cost the employee $6,800 ($1300 in premiums plus $5,000 toward the deductible and 10% of costs after deductible, which is $500). The middle deductible plan will cost the employee $6,650 ($2600 in premiums plus $3,000 toward the deductible and 15% of costs after deductible, which is $1,050).

YES: An employee who projects no medical costs should choose the plan with the lowest premium, and that is the high deductible plan, which costs the employee $1,300 a year.

YES: The high deductible plan will cost the employee $16,300, which is the lowest cost. This includes the $1,300 paid toward the premium, $5,000 toward the deductible, and 10% of $100,000, which equals $10,000 paid toward costs after the deductible.

3. A: The cost of tuition is increasing by 1% next year, which means that for an out-of-state resident, the cost per credit hour is $1,060.50. If a student takes 12 credit hours but then receives a 15% discount, the total tuition is 85% of $12,726, which is $10,817.10. This amount rounded to the nearest dollar is $10,817.

4. NO: Both students are taking fewer than 11 credit hours, so they both enroll on the third Monday in April.

NO: Students who take more than 7 credit hours next year will actually see their tuition decrease due to the new discounts.

YES: An in-state student taking 19 credit hours will pay $9,453.60 for the first 18 credit hours and $656.50 for the 19th credit hour, which totals $10,110.10

Graphic Interpretation

5. B: There are 15 employees out of 45 total employees that have worked at the company between 5 and 10 years. Therefore, the percentage is $\frac{15}{45} = 33.3\%$, rounded to the nearest tenth.

6. B: The car is traveling at a speed of 5 meters per second. On the interval from 1 to 3 seconds, the position changes by 10 meters. This is 10 meters in 2 seconds, or 5 meters in each second.

7. D: Because there are 267 seniors that are planning on going to school full time next year and that equals 53.9% of the total senior class, there are $267 \div 0.539 = 495$ total seniors at Heights High, rounded to the nearest integer. That means that 6.1% of 495 seniors are headed into the military, which equals $495 \times 0.061 = 30$, rounded.

8. B: The regression line predicts the output, given a specific input. Therefore, to approximate the miles driven in 7 hours, locate 7 on the x-axis, which corresponds to time. Then, locate the regression line at that x-value and find its corresponding y-value. Its corresponding y-value is approximately 57, which refers to 57 miles.

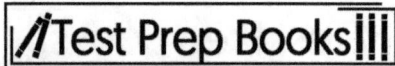

Answer Explanations #2

Two-Part Analysis

9. The correct value for x is 1296 and the correct value for y is 72 because $\frac{1296}{72} = 18$, which is a multiple of 9 because:

$$2 \times 9 = 18$$

10. There are 1,350 total business majors. Let a represent the number of accounting majors, and therefore the algebraic expression $3a$ can represent the number of marketing majors because there are 3 times as many accounting majors as marketing majors. There are 50 double majors. Therefore, we have the equation $1350 = a + 3a - 50$, which represents the total number of business majors. Subtracting the 50 represents any double-counting of double majors. Solving for a results in $a = 350$ the number of accounting majors. Therefore $3a = 1050$, the number of marketing majors. Therefore, the correct value for accounting is 350 and the correct value for marketing is 1,050.

Table Analysis

11. FALSE: The total number of basic packages sold was 135,800. However, dividing this amount by 4 results in an average of 33,950.

FALSE: The total number of non-basic packages sold was 251,100, and the total number of packages sold was 386,900, which is a percentage of 65%.

TRUE: The region with the largest number of internet sales for the ABC Cable Company was the Midwest. Totaling up the number of packages for each region results in the largest total for the Midwest region, 121,300 packages.

12. FALSE: The average number of credit hours completed was 15.3, which rounds to 15.

FALSE: Given the sample, the probability that a student is an engineering major is equal to the probability that a student is a physical therapy major because there were the same number of both majors in the sample.

FALSE: The data set corresponding to ACT scores has one mode, which is 31. It appears 3 times in the data set. No other score appears 3 times, so there is only one mode. A data set that is bimodal has 2 modes.

13. TRUE: Percent change is calculated by taking the ratio in change in population from year to year over the previous amount. For instance, from 2001 to 2002, the percent change is $\frac{301.2-300.1}{300.1} \times 100 = 0.366\%$, which rounds up to .37%. The population increased .37%. The year with the largest change occurred from 2002 to 2003, with a .43% decrease in population.

FALSE: The largest percent increase occurred from 2001 to 2002. The largest percent decrease occurred from 2002 to 2003.

TRUE: The population increased 0.38% from 2007 to 2008 and decreased 0.38% from 2004 to 2005.

Answer Explanations #2

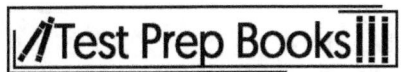

Data Sufficiency

14. B: Statement (1) is insufficient. We need to know how many packages there are total to find the number of potential selections. (A) and (D) are not possibilities. Statement (2) is sufficient. If there are 10 packages available and 4 possible selections, there are:

$$\binom{10}{4} = \frac{10 \times 9 \times 8 \times 7}{4 \times 3 \times 2} = 210 \text{ combinations}$$

15. A: Statement (1) states that Katie can finish the story in 4 hours, which means that Serena can finish the story in 8 hours because Katie is twice as fast as Serena. Because both of these quantities create rates, together they can finish one story in:

$$\frac{1}{4} + \frac{1}{8} = \frac{2}{8} + \frac{1}{8} = \frac{3}{8}$$

Dividing 8 by 3 shows that together they can finish the story in $2\frac{2}{3}$ hours. Therefore (1) is sufficient. Statement (2) is insufficient because we do not know how long the story is that they need to complete.

16. B: Statement (1) is insufficient. If x is a multiple of 6, it could be equal to 24. $9 - \frac{24}{9}$ does not result in an integer. Not all multiples of 6 are divisible by 9. Statement (2) is sufficient. Because $\frac{x}{9}$ has a remainder of 0, that means x is a multiple of 9 and the division results in an integer. An integer subtracted from 9, which is an integer, results in an integer.

17. D: Statement (1) is sufficient. Because there is a 25% profit on each box, oatmeal is sold for:

$$\$2 + 0.25 \times \$2 = \$2 + \$0.50 = \$2.50$$

Statement (2) is also sufficient. Because your selling price is 80% of your purchase price, $\$2 = 0.8 \times p$, where p is the purchase price. Therefore, $p = \frac{\$2}{.8} = \$2.50$. Both statements (1) and (2) are sufficient individually.

18. E: Statement (1) is not sufficient. If the mean is 3, then the sum of values is 21. If the median is 3, the middle of the values is 3. Neither one answers the question. Statement (2) is not sufficient. Knowing how many times the mode appears does not help us determine whether the median is less than the mode.

19. C: Statement (1) is insufficient by itself because it does not give us the height or radius of the cylinder. Statement (2) tells us that the base is 77 square centimeters, so its base is 7 by 11 centimeters. Therefore, the height is the third dimension: 12 centimeters. This is enough information to obtain the radius from the surface area given in (1). The height and radius are necessary to determine the volume of the cylinder. Therefore, both statements are sufficient together.

20. C: Statement (1) is insufficient because we need to know how many red marbles there are and it tells us that there are 14 blue marbles. Statement (2) tells us that the probability of selecting a green marble is equal to the probability of selecting a blue marble. Therefore, the number of blue marbles equals the number of green marbles, which is given to us as 14 in statement 1. Because there are 39

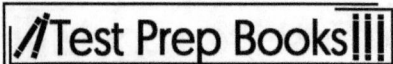

total marbles, that means 11 are red. Together, both statements enable us to find the probability of selecting a red marble as 11/39.

Index

Addition, 10, 12, 17, 83
Articles, 44
Average, 16, 50, 51, 59, 63, 68, 72, 73, 83, 84, 89, 93, 94, 97, 115, 118, 122
Base, 12, 23, 44, 61, 62, 82, 109, 123
Bias, 28, 34, 117
Cancel, 11, 15, 84, 110
Cause and Effect, 29, 60, 80
Common Denominator, 10, 11, 16, 74
Comparison-Contrast, 28, 29
Complex Sentence, 29
Conclusion, 31, 48, 75, 78, 79, 96, 116, 117, 118, 120
Counter-Argument, 31
Decimal Number, 12, 13
Decimal Place, 12, 13
Decimal Point, 12, 13, 21, 72
Decimal System, 12
Denominator, 10, 11, 13, 14, 19, 23, 74, 75, 112
Dependent, 119
Descriptive, 29, 57, 58
Difference, 10, 11, 17, 21, 50, 65, 74, 82, 83, 120
Divide Into One Another, 11
Dividend, 11, 13
Division, 11, 13, 17
Divisor, 11, 13
Essential, 59, 78
Estimation, 12, 15
Examples, 16, 19, 21, 22, 27, 28, 30, 31, 76, 116
Explanation, 28, 79, 80, 118
Expository, 28
Fact, 34, 75, 76, 119
First-Person Point of View, 29
Flashback, 32
Generalization, 60
Image, 29, 76, 91, 92, 93, 115
Improper Fraction, 11
Inference, 32
Introduction, 28, 30, 57
Inversely Proportional, 15
Irregular, 59, 79
Jargon, 28
Logical Fallacy, 34
Main, 28, 29, 30, 31, 32, 55, 75, 76, 94, 97, 116, 117, 118
Mean, 16, 29, 72, 108, 114, 123
Mixed Number, 11, 74, 75
Mood, 58
Multiplication, 10, 13, 17
Narrative, 27
Numerator, 10, 11, 19, 23, 72, 74, 75
Ordinary Average, 16
Paraphrasing, 30, 32
Percent, 13, 14, 15, 16, 21, 69, 74, 83, 99, 102, 103, 122
Persuasive, 27, 28
Phrase, 13, 118
Plane, 26
Point of View, 29, 30
Points, 26, 31, 32, 58, 76, 77, 83, 104, 117
Positive, 23, 43, 59, 63, 92, 115
Predictions, 32
Problem-Solution, 29
Product, 10, 43, 44, 45, 86, 87, 99, 110, 112
Proper Fraction, 11
Proportional, 15
Pythagorean Formula, 26
Quotient, 11, 17, 48, 55, 56, 76, 88, 104
Ratio, 15, 20, 93, 94, 115, 116, 122
Reciprocal, 11
Rectangle, 15
Regular, 59, 62, 81
Repeating, 12, 82
Rounding, 15
Second-Person Point of View, 30
Sequence, 28, 32, 57
Similar, 19, 43, 47, 57, 58, 77, 78, 114, 117, 118, 119, 120
Simplified, 11, 14, 22, 23, 73, 88, 112
Square, 15, 21, 85, 109, 113, 123
Subject, 29, 30, 33, 35, 91, 101, 114
Subtraction, 10, 13, 17
Sum, 10, 16, 17, 51, 73, 85, 123
Summarizing, 31
Supporting Details, 30, 31
Technical, 27, 28
Terminating, 12

Textual Evidence, 31
Thesis Statement, 30
Third-Person Limited, 30
Third-Person Objective, 30
Third-Person Omniscient, 30
Third-Person Point of View, 29

Tone, 35
Topic, 28, 30, 33, 35, 44, 81
Translation, 93, 94, 115
Weighted Average, 16
Weighted Mean, 16

Dear GMAT Focus Edition Test Taker,

Thank you for purchasing this study guide for your GMAT Focus Edition exam. We hope that we exceeded your expectations.

Our goal in creating this study guide was to cover all of the topics that you will see on the test. We also strove to make our practice questions as similar as possible to what you will encounter on test day. With that being said, if you found something that you feel was not up to your standards, please send us an email and let us know.

We would also like to let you know about other books in our catalog that may interest you.

GRE

This can be found on Amazon: amazon.com/dp/B0CJLCZVCS

MCAT

amazon.com/dp/B0CHD1KGPG

We have study guides in a wide variety of fields. If the one you are looking for isn't listed above, then try searching for it on Amazon or send us an email.

Thanks Again and Happy Testing!
Product Development Team
info@studyguideteam.com

FREE Test Taking Tips Video/DVD Offer

To better serve you, we created videos covering test taking tips that we want to give you for FREE. **These videos cover world-class tips that will help you succeed on your test.**

We just ask that you send us feedback about this product. Please let us know what you thought about it—whether good, bad, or indifferent.

To get your **FREE videos**, you can use the QR code below or email freevideos@studyguideteam.com with "Free Videos" in the subject line and the following information in the body of the email:

    a. The title of your product

    b. Your product rating on a scale of 1-5, with 5 being the highest

    c. Your feedback about the product

If you have any questions or concerns, please don't hesitate to contact us at info@studyguideteam.com.

Thank you!

www.ingramcontent.com/pod-product-compliance
Lightning Source LLC
Chambersburg PA
CBHW080552230426
43663CB00015B/2811